When I See The
Wild GOD

About the Author

Ly de Angeles has been an initiated priestess for many years. She is High Priestess of an Australian coven known as Coven Crystalglade, and has been involved in the occult arts and sciences since her introduction to it when she was a young girl.

The author of several books, Ly is a worldwide Tarot consultant and has taught Tarot and similar occult subjects for years.

To Write to the Author

If you wish to contact the author or would like more information about this book, please write to the author in care of Llewellyn Worldwide and we will forward your request. Both the author and publisher appreciate hearing from you and learning of your enjoyment of this book and how it has helped you. Llewellyn Worldwide cannot guarantee that every letter written to the author can be answered, but all will be forwarded. Please write to:

Ly de Angeles
℅ Llewellyn Worldwide
P.O. Box 64383, Dept. 0-7387-0576-4
St. Paul, MN 55164-0383, U.S.A.

Please enclose a self-addressed stamped envelope for reply, or $1.00 to cover costs. If outside U.S.A., enclose international postal reply coupon.

Many of Llewellyn's authors have websites with additional information and resources. For more information, please visit our website at:

http://www.llewellyn.com

When I See The Wild GOD

encountering urban celtic witchcraft

LY DE ANGELES

2004
Llewellyn Publications
St. Paul, Minnesota 55164-0383, U.S.A.

First Edition
First Printing, 2004

Cover design by Gavin Dayton Duffy
Cover photograph © 2004, Ron VanZee Photography
Edited by Karin Simoneau
Interior art by Llewellyn art department
Wild God mask created by Monica Roxburgh, Goblin Art

Library of Congress Cataloging-in-Publication Data
de Angeles, Ly, 1951–
   When I see the wild god: encountering urban Celtic witchcraft / Ly de Angeles.
     p. cm.
   Includes bibliographical references.
   ISBN 0-7387-0576-4
    1. Witchcraft. 2. Celts—Religion—Miscellanea. I. Title.

BF1566.D37 2004
299'.94—dc22   2004040837

Llewellyn Publications
A Division of Llewellyn Worldwide, Ltd.
P.O. Box 64383, Dept. 0-7387-0576-4
St. Paul, MN 55164-0383, U.S.A.
www.llewellyn.com

 Printed in the United States of America on recycled paper

Be warned, daughter. He will use all his strength against you,
and his strength is formidable. He will fight you every step of the way.
It's a cruel task, for you must unfasten the bindings of his heart and lay it bare.
There's great pain there; a pain he does not want to share with you.

—Juliet Marillier, from *Son of the Shadows*

Other Books by Ly de Angeles

Witchcraft: Theory and Practice
The Feast of Flesh and Spirit
Genesis: A Legend of Future Past

Contents

Acknowledgments

My thanks to some of the great Seanachaì [shan-ukh-ee] of the current era (in alphabetical order): Marion Bradley, Charles de Lint, Kenneth Flint, Morgan Llywelyn, Caiseal Mór, Sherri S. Tepper, and Terri Windling.

The music of Willie McElroy and the Wild Zinnias—Byron Bay's own local Irish folk-rock band—Jethro Tull, Loreena McKennitt, Clannad, the Chieftains, Dead Can Dance, Filippa Giordano, Sinéad O'Connor.

The artwork of Brian Froud.

The initiates and allies of the Coven, and my family, related by blood and otherwise—particularly Ren and Josh, for listening.

And Hunter, Brighid, and the Fianna, for coming when you did!

These people keep magic in the world.

Preface

The cairn of dolmen stones—mosses and lichens covering the swirls and patterns that mark a forgotten ancestry—stands silent and brooding upon the barren hilltop, sentinels that guard an ancient Gate that opens onto elsewhere.

Today draws to a close, but the signs of summer, subtle as they are, can be seen, felt, and heard all around.

The sun dips toward the western horizon, creating mysterious depths and hollows within the rough circle of still-warm stones as they cast their long shadows upon the ground.

I always wake from the sleep of the light between the sunset and the dark, when the world gets just a little calmer. At first glance the place seems empty, its stillness unbroken, its ancient unseen power thrumming quietly within itself.

But then I see him move (he was not a shadow after all).

A huge dark man, dressed as though he were a ragged crow—with dreds that fall in a cascade, all threaded here and there with blackbird feathers that catch the fading light in their blue-black sheen—stands as still as the stones themselves, facing into the sunset. I see him from my silent watching place and know at once just who he is.

The ancient man, Hunter, blessed of the fair folk. I smile. He is still alive, despite how many folk have tried to cut him down.

It's been a long, long time since he has come to my Gate. A thousand years or more spent wandering the ancient trackways to remind the earth that she is precious and that he guards her still. I sense the others not far away and I know they'll keep the fires burning against a night not mine—not clean.

At the moment of the sun's disappearance, in a splash of molten gold, in a crimson and pale mauve sky, he raises his arms and begins a low, strong, beautiful song. The words are in the old tongue—potent—meant to evoke yearning in the memories of those who think themselves forgotten.

Darkness now hastens to claim its own time, and as the last of the light fades into dusk Hunter turns to face inward into the Ring, bringing the calling to a close.

I can't read his thoughts, but I understand the sad and haunted light behind his black, steady gaze. Ah, well, there's all the time of the night to hear his story. It's fortunate indeed that I am here now.

He pauses a moment before he moves to close the circle in the Ring, shutting out the other world.

Night has almost fully spun its web of deeper mystery, and I sense the feelings of loss, and relentless determination in the face of so much tragedy, that dwell behind the iron-strong discipline. The draíocht of the Lord of Life and Death, the fire of inspiration, all the legends and the patterns and the spells—the whole of him . . . yeah, I know it also. For I am the Watcher. And he knows that I am here—but I'm not the one he seeks.

The moon is rising now, above the sacred stone that is his altar, and she casts her silver glow into the Ring. The familiar scene becomes unearthly and filled with the older mysteries.

This is the time between.

This is the time, in ages past, when he would normally leave, abandoning the shrine to the dark, to travel in that other world along with the pack he calls "the band," searching for the lost, or the hated—their fate determined by the scent that they emit.

Yet this one time he remains—motionless, watchful, waiting. I hear his breathing as it becomes a little faster, just a little harder, as the presences other than both of us arrive—guardians of the stones and whisperers of ancient magic older still than any of us.

There! Within the deep shadows of the farthest dolmen arch, a small figure—robed, it would seem, from the swirling darkness itself; a darkening and thickening of the shadows, and as black as the deepest, sunless sky.

The figure walks into the Ring and he sees that it is, perhaps, a woman's form, though whether mortal or sídhe, or the one he seeks, he cannot tell.

In his customary quiet voice, he asks, "Are you . . . ?"

She smiles and moves, and from within the dark folds of her cloak, tiny, brilliant points of light shine and twinkle like stars within blackness, mists roil and swirl like forgotten ghosts, and a murder of ravens swoops from the depths with a rattle of wings and a hundred conversations, to fly, mad and carefree upon the wind, to places in the mortal world—messengers, oracles—to those who still know how to read the signs.

"You know me, Hunter." Her voice is soft and deep. "I am the hidden depths. I am silence, and patience, and stillness. I am the dark womb and the peaceful tomb and we are one. I am the bare bones of all that is, and I am the time it takes to crumble them to dust, and the earth that claims them for her garden.

"I am the quiet stone and the rich, damp soil beneath their feet. I am the mystery of the dark and bottomless well wherein they look for visions.

"I am the longing and the hunger for what they think they have forfeited."

"I'm okay," sighs Hunter, the things he's seen laid open for her to know, for no other could look and not be frightened for the future.

"I'm your grail, Hunter—you know that. Drink deeply of my draíocht, and know the taste of me upon your lips, because it's not over yet for us—we are still here, and therefore life continues.

"I'm tired, Lady . . ." says Hunter, finally able to relax the burden of keeping wonder alive within a tangle of human disdain.

"Be with me a while. This night. Tread the steps of the dance of a new day, so that you might feel the pleasure of forgetting for a moment—a little gift I'm good at! And so that I can breathe the forest that I smell upon you.

"We all pay homage to the dance of life and death, so let us dance it fearlessly, for does not this earth, these rocks and stones who listen so intently, invite us?

"In the morning you'll remember that to each of us, and everything, there is bequeathed a time and purpose. Your purpose is not opposed to mine, nor mine to yours, for there is no day without night—and where, I ever wonder, is there thought of separation?"

"And herein lies the Mystery . . ." says Hunter, smiling.

"It's love, Hunter. You know about love?"

"Yeah, I know about that, Lady."

The wind rises and carries the distant sound, first of Matt's piping, then Willie's fiddle, then Alan's bodhrán.

I smile. These folk are mine!

Introduction

Two roads diverged in a wood, and I—
I took the one less travelled by,
and that has made all the difference.

—Robert Frost

For witches just beginning the long journey, there is an already extensive array of books in print that fully discuss the goddesses and the rites that connect you to her seasons, and it is a "done deal" that you will study them, as no witch is complete without knowing her. However, without a deep understanding of her Brother/Son/King/Consort/Champion—the witch's God—the world is a sad and unbalanced place, as the monotheistic hegemony of "the one true god" has too many people fooled.

Witchcraft and the Draiocht

To know myself, therefore to be *real* in the way I live in the ways of magic, it's been a necessary (and passionate) journey of learning what is important in relation to what I study and how I live. It's been necessary to constantly question what I've learned *and* what I teach others, and to make changes if necessary.

Why? Because too many eyes and minds, aware of the effects of the "modern day" and the current history, are blind to the Big Picture—our effects on Forever and Forever's effects upon us.

I sense the Déithe around me all the time. They speak to me—through wind and rain, birdcall, the attitude of animal and ant, especially via the moods of the sea, mists in valleys, the seasons' smells. They speak to me through the words in my mind and the words of others spoken or written, through dreams, visions, and omens.

This work aims to aid you in three ways: it will help you become self-aware *as* a witch, assist you with the ritual and magic of witchcraft, and, thirdly, provide you with an access into the worlds of magic by way of specific stories (scéalta) and legends that act as guides into these worlds.

This work is intended as an adjunct to *Witchcraft: Theory and Practice,* published by Llewellyn Worldwide. You will find specific disciplines and fundamental techniques within its pages if you choose to read it.

You either will, or have, spent many years exploring history, mythology, the legends, and ways of the sacred of the people of the world, and much of your study will be through the use of the written word.

You'll also spend years contemplating Forever—the Songline (the word is the expression of forever and our inter-connection with our living environment, used by the indigenous people of Australia); Imramma (loosely, *wonder-voyage,* the forever-journey of the scéalta); and time—and what, if anything, "the gods" are. You'll want to feel connected. You'll think you are connected. Truth is, you *are* connected. To what? Everything.

Celtic Draiocht

This book presents (mainly) a Celtic perspective of sacredness. Even though our blood is distributed throughout the world and has mingled with that of many peoples, it is a very ancient blood that aligns us with a "native" inheritance, suppressed almost to extinction by oppressive regimes of conquest. It is requested that this Mythos be understood through alliance with your geographic location, through connecting with your present environment and that environment's indigenous people, and in respect of those indigenous people and their rights to self-determination: this tends to form a great tapestry of world understanding that needs to be seen through the wider vision and not the simple glance.

The traditions of our Celtic palingenesis are a wealth of draíocht and creativity. Knowing them allows us to honor and acknowledge not only our past histories in the light of what *probably* occurred (in at least some greater accuracy than has generally been presumed by those who wrote, and subsequently taught, the history by and on behalf of the conquerors), but our own present draíocht and spiritual traditions that are available to us by the very nature of genetics (blood and spirit in continuum).

No matter where in the world you may live, many of us share a common "religion" that pre-dates the onset of Christianity by thousands of years; the earth's people are really extremely tribal, still, despite technological and scientific representation.

Our common Celticness is not bound by geography but by racial memory ("a dog can be born in a stable but that doesn't make it a horse"). We can love and honor the lands in which we live—and we have our own unique tribal lineage to integrate with those lands—but we cannot assume some illusory "higher authority" over those who are indigenous to those lands; we must seek only to share what we are and what we know, which is, in many cases, that of a Celtic heritage.

Aligning with our origins—our blood—is like a line of least resistance that opens "doorways" by its very recognition.

This work gives examples of many of the Gods of Eire (Ireland) and Cymru (Wales). They have come through time without much interference from invaders, in difference to Albion (now called England), which bore the brunt of ceaseless incursions by Romans, Saxons, Angles, Jutes, and Normans, resulting in the transformation of the identities of the gods and goddesses, seemingly replacing them with the Arthurian Mythos on which I have leaned for the sake of familiarity.

Each of these aspects (personas) has its own legends and myths, which I suggest that you research and study in your own time; this is not necessary to the purpose here.

These persona are a later rendering of earlier traditions, many of which I will name so that you can explore Imramma by comprehending these legends also.

I'm sure those of you who are fey with other lineages can adapt the work accordingly. It won't take much effort to find the gods of other pantheons and work with them, as there are many branches of the World Tree, and many similar understandings of that which is sacred.

May it serve.

Part I

A Living Craft

Witchcraft in a Noisy World

And the sign said, The words of the prophets
are written on the subway walls
And tenement halls.
And whispered in the sounds of silence.

—Simon and Garfunkel, "The Sound of Silence"

Logos

We are bombarded, daily, by the Great God Logos—the Word.

I listen to Lee Lin Chin or Mary Kostakidas (SBS World News) as they tell of the (edited) events of the day and the events' current implications for humanity.

And that's it, isn't it? The news is all about people: what people do to people; what the weather is doing to people; how people are creating the greenhouse effect; how many people and their homes are affected by fire, flood, famine, drought; or else it's about the economy (another species that is as sick or as healthy as people).

And the news is mostly tragic.

When you hear or read or talk about the news of the world, do you fear? Do you anticipate?

What do you talk about with your family? What do you talk about with your friends or your peers? What do you talk about with your lovers? How often do you agree or disagree? How often do you agree or disagree with each other regarding the opinions of others?

It's important to consider what we say, how we say it, *why* we say what we do; it's important to consider what we listen to, why we listen to it.

It's always personal, you know—our connectedness to the Big Picture.

But so often the Big Picture is perceived as recent and not in the context of its foreverness.

We're assaulted by advertising, by investment strategies, by the requirement to assist the economy by consuming, by a seeming world-need to achieve, strive, guard against, impress, gain, be entertained, and to fit in.

It all becomes quite deafening.

Logos (words) trigger war and they implore for peace. They can soothe or they can interfere. They can be spoken or written for the sake of being spoken or written. They can manipulate, but they can also educate.

I love words, but I deplore too many of them or (often) the ways in which they are used. Ah! But that's not the fault of the words themselves, is it? That blame can be laid at the feet of those who use them without care as to the effect they could have! And it's because of who those people *are* and the *Mythos* through which they perceive life that we cannot see eye to eye.

Mythos

- The Seen-Real: first world—the day to day, Otherworld

- The Unseen-Real: second world (until we're there)

- The Seen-Real: second world also (when we're in it)

Mythos is a plethora of many "worlds" all interconnected. People can (and do) inhabit more than one world: the guy down on the floor of the stock exchange jabbing at the air and yelling can be fully immersed in the Mythos of that world. Then he goes home. He eats a little, then showers and changes into his ritual garments, casts a Circle with his athame, and transports himself into his other world; his other Mythos . . .

. . . and this world is *not* the same as the first world mentioned above. They overlap, surely, and each affects the other. What *is* the same is one who walks between them—the one who travels both of them. When this person enters into the Mythos of magic, he or she enters into a world where time, as is generally thought, does not exist.

Mythos can only ever be experienced and understood as a result of that experience. It changes us . . . and words don't matter.

Logos can assist us to access the Worlds of Mythos (which is what this book's about), but words themselves can never take you there. You go there because you already co-exist with these worlds, and Logos can act as the mirror into which you peer to seek your own reflection.

The second world—the Mythos of magic (which you will find throughout this book is called *draíocht*)—is as experiential as the world of the floor of the stock exchange to the man who knows them both, but the traveler who walks the second world journeys from the Seen-Real (the stock exchange) and contemplates the Unseen-Real (the image of the second world), whereby it becomes the Seen-Real (because he's experiencing it).

What happens to us, as a result of traveling between one Mythos and another, is that we change. Not only do *we* change, but the world (that others think of, perhaps, as the *only* world in existence) changes also. It's as though we trail filaments of the places through which we travel back into the day to day, affecting it and changing it a little at a time.

Creativity, in all its many guises and expressions, is the result of these journeys into the Unseen-Real and of bridging Mythos to Mythos.

Do you ever wonder why so many books that were written in the past and claim to be futuristic, fantasy, or science fiction actually, from the viewpoint of the present, seem prophetic?

This book is essentially about accessing the experience of Mythos.

2   Forever and the Song of Earth

A human being . . . experiences himself, his thoughts and feelings,
as separated from the rest—a kind of optical delusion of consciousness.
This delusion is a kind of prison for us, restricting us to our personal
desires and to affections for a few persons nearest to us.

—Albert Einstein

Mythos is a way of expressing and experiencing forever in a "time and place" scenario. That's easy to do because you live forever and experience everything. One small part of living forever is the body of the person you are now.

Do you know that you've been alive Forever? That the memory of Forever is encoded into every cell of the body of you? That the hydrogen atom, the iron atom, the mitochondrial DNA that expresses the pattern of you, now, and the flora and fauna living and breeding in your gut and on your skin (and everywhere else on/in you) has lived forever; has always been somewhere?

You can access that Forever, you know. You can remember. Your "humanness" might be the merging of many cultures, many bloodlines, and through the study of the many-colored tapestry of culture, history, myth, and legend, you'll see yourself; you'll feel the connection—maybe to just one or two places, maybe to many, and perhaps to certain specific myths and legends.

These are your inheritance, you within the Songline, you upon the journey of Imramma.

This connection is to the Song of the Earth and to our place within the Song. Our awareness of this Song is very, very important—and it hasn't any words. No Logos. It is Earth's (unheard-with-ears) Song of Forever and it can only ever be felt or sensed.

Words can mimic the Song (by way of their harmony and placement) or they can be dust and discord.

The *way* each person lives is the way he or she merges with the Song. The way of magic is about merging with the Song, "hearing" it and acting accordingly.

The Song is nonjudgmental. It has no moralistic premise or attitude. It neither condemns nor condones, is neither "good" nor "bad," it just *is,* and therefore it is the truth.

People often try to interpret the Song according to pre-set parameters or previously considered philosophies, and this is a bias that's very difficult to drop; it is, however, worth both knowing *and* dropping.

There are limited evaluations of "right" and "wrong" (what the world of "people" is doing/what the world of "nature" is doing—somehow dividing them into two separate, often opposing categories), and there is the unlimited Big Picture (life forever—suns and stars and space beyond measure).

Time-out to contemplate the Big Picture?

You can realize that personally—individually—you (we) are probably *irrelevant.* Ah! So then, this being realized, you (we) can get on with a life of living well, of doing what is considered important, regardless of recognition or the lack of it, because you might as well!

No one can *really* tell you what's right or wrong; you can't *not* know! You *do* know! For yourself, for those around you, for life itself, which is so intensely precious. You know it all innately . . .

. . . because once you've contemplated (and sort of understood) the Big Picture, forever, the Song, how Logos operates, your life in the unlimited Worlds of Mythos, you can make conscious choices.

Magic is all about conscious choices, walking the many worlds, fixing what you can fix (because it feels innately right to do so), changing what you *can* change (ditto), and it is *all* about walking with the gods (when you've discovered what they are).

Of Gods and Goddesses

Witchcraft reinforces, in our culture, the honor and awareness of a Goddess (for lack of a better word). This means all kinds of things to many different people, but nothing even remotely limited to a human construct to me.

Witchcraft is also, most assuredly, aware of God (for lack of any other suitable analogy), although not in the way that most religions are.

I do not personally like either the word "goddess" or the word "god," as these words are "loaded." Preconceptions are consistently able to reinforce stereotyping, and it can be so easy to fall into age-worn patterns of externalization or exclusivity. We can call them by these two words, but I suggest that we do not become complacent.

Throughout this book I will constantly refer to them as *he, she, them,* and, when referring to a name of God I will refer to him in the collective, using the older Gaeilge equivalent for "gods": *Déithe*, always plural, therefore embracing all the gods-in-common or those expressing the same/similar traits (for example, when I refer to the Déithe *Merlin*, I inform you that many gods are the same/similar, such as Math, Gwyn ap Nudd, Ogmios, Urien, and Arawn, for all the gods are not one God, but rather many gods known by several names [depending on the pantheon], expressing variations of a theme by way of their attributes, personalities, and exploits).

When referring to the Goddess throughout this book I will be calling her Déithe, *and* by the title/name Mórrigan (which means "Great Queen"), for I am her priestess.

Animism, Pantheism, and the Ancestral Nature of Witchcraft

Anima

The vital principle; source of energy and creative action; soul; life.

Pantheon

All the gods of a people, collectively.

Witchcraft is very much a process of integrating our awareness of our-selves—as a species—with *everything else,* removing the false sense of iso-lation and inequality that is humanity's angst at its psychological alien-ation from the Big Picture (life, forever, and everything).

So how do we understand what a "goddess" is? What a "god" is? Two ways: one's personal; the other is by interconnection—the understanding that nothing is disconnected from anything else.

This understanding, of course, is how magic happens.

Women who are witches have the knowledge of the many representa-tions (aspects, mythologies, interpretations, psychologies) of the Mórrigan at their fingertips, as well as others of equal potency, and they are con-fronted by her in every recorded pantheon, thanks to the work of many people over the past several decades. These priestesses see themselves reflected in one or another of her humanized or totemic representations, and work at invoking and interpreting her through empathy with the per-sona to which they are most attuned. They have the cycles of the moon to guide them, the cycles of their own bodies, and, through the countless years of suppression, the determination to express individuality in not only relationships but also society as a whole.

Generally, there are more women owning up to being witches than men, but that's changing as the taboos are seen for what they are. And witches *know* that that's what they are. Men who are not witches cannot (do not) understand about men who *are* witches, so how easy is it to pub-licly proclaim oneself?

Much of this is the fault of "Western" culture, as a "rite of passage" does not exist for boys or men, and they are under constant pressure from their peers to conform, usually to their detriment (the men who apply these pressures are men who do not understand the ways of women sufficiently to interrelate through mutual respect of our intrinsic differences), and many men who *are* witches and who seek initiation into an established coven are put on immediate defensive by women trained as priestesses (unless the men are used to the women!).

The men who *do* seek initiation as priest/witch have an advantage that holds them in good stead—they know what they want to do, and it is very much the right of the Mórrigan to work with her brothers, lovers, sons, and champions to enable them to learn how they can gain, and give, all the insights and knowledge available, through both honoring her and resonating and representing our gods (by any or many of their names and purposes) themselves, both personally and collectively.

We are the offspring (or an expression) of Déithe—of life. We're one of the many ways that Déithe manifest themselves within life, and as such we revere the sacredness inherent in all things and seek to interweave our lives with the so-called tapestry of the Evolving Whole. Unlike other religions, we do this by answering to the call of the *wildness* in ourselves as well as heeding the so-called "civilized."

We are of the earth; we are physical; we learn all about birth, life, and death, and seek to give each of these passages its due respect. Turning one's face "heavenward" and denying the significance of a life well-lived *now,* and all that this signifies, is the cause of the harm that we see being perpetrated at earth's expense, and all that she is, right now. This degradation cannot be tolerated and should not be condoned. Our biological species is responsible and will be accountable for its negligence.

Working draíocht is working with our innate inheritance. Working *with* the forces of life instead of seemingly against them provides us with a common purpose: to work the draíocht, to defend what is threatened, to keep the arts of magic alive for future generations.

This work presents symbolic legends and practical disciplines, introducing you to the many persona of the witch's gods and the rites and rituals of a practicing male witch: a Cunning Man. The training herein is specifically for you.

These workings are seemingly directed toward heterosexual men. Gay witches are asked to realize that all the people, animals, plants, and everything, within each legend, represents you. You probably won't need to adapt the legends, but do so if you choose.

Throughout this book most ritual incorporates visual story. These are to be read and understood, insofar as they not only represent you (every character—man, woman, plant, animal, whatever), but also, through their Mythos, nature itself.

You will find yourself understanding not only yourself, but other men, women, and the draíocht that represent the Mórrigan and all Déithe of the priesthood of witchcraft.

Each legend is a ritual journey into one of the Worlds of Mythos.

The many invocations ("That which I adore I also invoke . . .") will open you up to the Imramma represented by the persona of Déithe, and you will integrate Déithe through your recognition of them; they connect you.

Jung considered these persona as *archetypes,* and this is true, but they are more, and other, than this: they dwell in your racial memory; they exist in nature as separate entities that can be known.

While knowing the Déithe of the Mórrigan and working her rites with the priestesses of the Craft at the full moon, dark moon, and new moon (when and if that happens), you may find, when working solitary, the need to tap into the Esbat ritual at the full of the moon only, until such time as you can "work" with a priestess. The more knowledge you have of these rituals, the more chance you will have, upon finding a priestess with whom to work, of reflecting to her the Mórrigan as *you* know her and of representing our Déithe within the rituals.

So, herein are solar/earth rituals that will begin your quest, the main aims of which are: to align yourself to the rites of a male witch, and to align yourself with the Mórrigan through acknowledgment and representation of her god, king, and consort (lover, friend, and ally).

The Ancestral Nature of Witchcraft

If you take such theories as the Big Bang into account (and it's as viable theory as any other if you feel the necessity to consider *anything* as having a beginning), then "we" must, logically, have been there, in the ancestral sense, as nothing comes from nothing, even if it is (in difference to "was"— I'm sure you'll work with me here!) merely as the possibility of energy as we consider energy to be. The same applies if you throw away the entire illusion of a beginning and consider the concept of a continuum, and consider the possibly that we don't know everything (consciously).

We're the offspring of that immortality. We may be sun and moon and sea and stone and person and rat and mountain lion and reto-virus and all, but we're still related! And everything is unique but relative to everything else ("divided for love's sake on the chance of union").

Witchcraft acknowledges this "deep-time" ancestry by our awareness of the very few degrees of difference between all things (certainly not just others of our own species), and honors the connections most specifically at the festival of Samhain.

3 The Sight

This might suggest that the so-called imaginary time is really the real time, and that which we call real time is just a figment of our imaginations.

—Stephen Hawking

Despite the Déithe being all around us in the world of the external senses, there is also The Secret "Outside." Within each of us is a seemingly limitless and constantly expansive world whereby the Déithe are met in one way—a way whereby we can mutually communicate, where the keys of knowledge and symbolism combine: *Creative Visualization* (conscious imagining).

A large percentage of social regimes prefer it if people don't think too much just in case positions of "authority" are questioned. Many religious regimes, of both the past and the present, *also* do not want us to think too much, in case we come up with questions that would conflict with their dogma ("control").

The "rational/logical" post-modern society of this and the last century has much to answer for when it tried (unsuccessfully) to belittle the greatest gift that the human mind has at its disposal—the imagination. This tool can be likened to several things: a transmitter and a receiver, a pool of inherited symbolic association, and, most important of all, the key faculty necessary in both knowing draíocht and realizing Déithe.

The use of controlled visualization (rather than idle meandering) *is* draíocht.

Understand symbolism (the language of draíocht), and break down conditioning.

In all situations where controlled visualization is practiced you will need to utilize your ability to "look it up" when things other than those you have "set up" come your way on the journeys.

The worlds of the elements (and meeting the Déithe that dwell there) are, at first consideration, easy to access. That "ease," however, can be misleading. Be wary of any egoistic interpretations of experience (being glamoured). The Déithe of the elements that inhabit these worlds are not, after all, human/mortal—they don't "do" in ways that we do. They simply are.

They are, collectively, Imramma and the Déithe (of nature), and they are influenced by whatever the "laws of nature" are, and are affected by everything we are affected by. We, as a (collective) species, have somehow got it into our heads that we are not subject to these laws, and so seek to control everything (!). This has led to the environmental madness that is decimating earth (and I sense that the Déithe are getting *really* upset at all this stupidity!).

This denial of the Laws of Change has also come close to closing off the access to the draíocht and the Worlds of Mythos, and this process must not be perpetuated. For the denial of these worlds would close down the inspiration necessary to amend the current abuse of our home (and that would be a little like the "Nothing" in the movie *The NeverEnding Story)*.

Our ability to walk between the worlds is our innate right, and it is our personal responsibility, as witches, to keep the draíocht "healthy."

> The problems of the world cannot possibly be solved by skeptics or cynics whose horizons are limited by the obvious realities. We need men who can dream of things that never were.
>
> —John F. Kennedy

Part 2

The Wheel of the Solar/Earth Year (1)

4
On Death, Life, and Timelessness

Do not go gentle into that good night,
. . . Rage, rage against the dying of the light.

—Dylan Thomas

Everybody wants immortality. Everybody wants to *know* that everything's going to work out fine and that everything's going to have a happy ending. Lots of people talk about the "light," about peace, about something like "nirvana," "heaven," "valhalla," dissolution, entropy. Some of us dream of Tir na n'Ogh (Isle of the Ever-young), Tir na Asarlai (Isle of the Mages), Tir na Taibhse (Isle of Ghosts—the Ancestors), or Hy Brasil (Isle of Dreams).

(We have all that—not later, but now. It depends on one's perspective.)

People seek that immortality through understanding not only our possible origins, but also our possible final endings.

Some talk about the End-of-Days, Armageddon, the Final Solution (muhahaha!).

People seek to understand Imramma by way of the theory of reincarnation, by way of recognizing our genetic/environmental blueprint, by seeking to comprehend the mechanics of biological life, or through seeking to comprehend how old life is (and what else the Big Bang might have been).

Many seek their spirituality through science, particularly quantum physics. The ancients had it right all along.

By understanding that "body-death" is not only natural but also unavoidable (what is compost, after all?), we can release any illusions of fear that we might just disappear. The bottom line is that it doesn't matter. There's nothing else *but* life. Nothing is outside of the Pattern (even that which is seemingly inert is merely slow).

This understanding is so draíochta. It is only our constantly current actions that matter. The intent and repercussions of these actions affect Forever. This is a responsibility, yes?

A man named Michael, who had been diagnosed with terminal cancer, asked me at one of my workshops to tell him about death, and what followed. He hated my answer. I told him that I would tell him when it happened to me (if I recognized it when it happened!). He considered the answer to be opting out of my responsibility as a teacher of things "occult and spiritual." And yet, it would have been extremely presumptuous of me to attempt to lift a veil that can only be lifted through personal experience.

People consider body-death, and what happens after the event, to be the Inner Sanctum of the Holy of Holies—quite often a taboo or closed subject. I like to talk about it; to contemplate it (even to think about microscopic organisms); to be okay with it. One can never fully understand an experience until it's personal—each has his or her own views, and speaking from desire does not necessarily have anything to do with the truth.

The theory and practice in this part of the book deals with transition, from one way of emoting and living to another. Isn't that life? Isn't it death?

5   The Celtic Cross

Came upon an ancient forest
A guiding power had led me there
Walking through the mystic forest
The legend, tale of times gone by.

—Clannad, "Ancient Forest"

The Elements

I'm presenting both common and Celtic considerations of each element, as well as an understanding of their environmental implications. Knowledge acquired through the use of elemental invocation is very necessary, for without it people can be out of balance with the Déithe, and if *we* are unbalanced, life is unbalanced (which is probably what is wrong with the world today!).

The Tuatha dé Danann and the Four Cities
A Brief Period of Intense Speculation

What makes a legend are those people or events that are so profound as to be remembered generation after generation more for what they represent to the collective consciousness than for the accuracy of their historicity.

So it is with the Tuatha dé Danann.

From the perspective of the current era they were considered as everything from a race of gods (or giants), to little winged fairies (I'll get back to *that* misnomer in a moment!), to simply another invading bunch of colonialists (misappropriating the tribal lands of the Firbolg).

They are reputed to have come from the "north," from Greece, from the sky—opinions differ everywhere—and they are said to have come from the vicinity of the Danube (hence Dana).

The Tuatha dé Danann were also said to have come from Four Great Cities and to have brought with them a treasure of renown from each of those cities: from Finias in the north they brought a spear (some obscure texts say it was a sling-shot—hmm . . .); from Gorias in the east they brought the sword; from Murias in the west, the Cauldron of Plenty (and rebirth); and from the south, Falias, they brought the famed Lia Fáil, the Stone of Truth and/or the Stone of Destiny, upon which the true kings of Ireland were said to have been acknowledged when the Stone cried out.

These Four Cities are both sacred and mythic. In truth no one knows where these cities were, on earth, or even *if* they were (historically).

That they represent the four cardinal directions is certain—hence, also, the four sacred treasures.

What is *always* agreed upon, by all who have handed the legends through the passage of time (even the Milesians and the Firbolg), is that the Tuatha dé Danann were brilliant—a "highly advanced" people gifted in the craft of enchantment and all things draíocht, all the arts, maritime and martial skills, metal-working, oratory, and, oh, just about everything! And it turned out that they were willing, once settled and at peace, to share what they knew with the locals.

There's also much speculation and guesswork regarding *when* (historically) they landed on the shores of Connaught, but the bottom line is— who knows for certain? The only form of written record that we have is Ogham, and that was only ever used by the Druids to keep certain records.

The Tuatha dé Danann, due to the subsequent invasion of the Milesians, are said to have gone underground, into the hills, into the hollow earth, into the hollow hills, or to have merged with the earth. They were said to have struck up a bond with the Milesians whereby they would rule the underworld and the Milesians could rule on earth, and as a bond of honor the Quicken Tree was planted (whose berries—rowan—were able to impart immortality) as a symbol of the continued alliance of the two peoples.

The Quicken Tree

Take time out to explore the sacredness of the Tree in as many cultures and societies as you can: the Quicken, Oak, Yggdrasil, and Asherah (also known as the Tree of Life) are a few among many trees (please see *Witchcraft: Theory and Practice,* pages 122–123) perceived as sacred *everywhere.*

The Quicken Tree was a rowan tree, but not just any rowan tree.

The magical properties of the rowan are those of protection, vision, and enchantment, and both the wood and the berries can be added to incense to aid the sight.

The rowan is sacred to the goddesses of fire—Brighid in Ireland and Brigantia of the Britons—and is said to "quicken" all things associated with the casting of enchantments and their manifestation.

In the wild, the rowan will grow higher up the sides of mountains than most other trees, sometimes growing from the tiniest of crevices in the most inaccessible of spots. Its life-force is strong and determined. It reflects power, vitality, and tenacity.

Rowan trees are planted at stone circles and dragon lines because they also provide powerful protection for sacred land and sacred places.

And now we come to the point.

The Quicken Tree was the symbol of agreement between two peoples—the Tuatha dé Danann and the Milesians—and while it stood it represented peace for the land. The berries were said to bestow sacred vision and immortality to those partaking of the Quicken Brew in a rite of passage that few survived. Only the berries of the Quicken Tree prevailed.

Enter the jealousy and resentment of a man who thought he should be king but was not chosen, and thus became determined to destroy the man who was. Resentment has a way of growing like a noxious weed into a full-blown psychic epidemic of consciousness, causing people to do the unthinkable, which is exactly what the thwarted man did. He chose to side with the enemies of his land in his quest to take what he had not won, and he waged war upon the king with the outsiders at his side.

They cut down the Tree.

There has been no peace since.

At the scene of the devastation were a brother and a sister, trained in the ways of the sacred mysteries of earth and sky and sea, and they managed to collect some of the berries . . .

Knowledge and history were preserved, and passed along the Imramma, down the generations, by way of stories, poetry, song, and music—by way of the amazing and awesome tribal tradition of social and genealogical memory (with a bit of help from the ancestors!).

Hence the berries of the Quicken Tree and the gift of immortality.

A Note on the Term "Fairy"

Please contemplate the following list: fairy (fair folk), faerie, fae, fey (fae—faer [archaic of "fear"]) faerie, faidh, fair, fate, fairly.

They are all variations on the same theme. "Fey" or "fae" means "able to cast enchantments." When you're "fairly sure," aren't you leaving room for the possibility of doubt (of the intervention of fate)? Doesn't the idea of fate give you that certain feeling? What about Morgan—Morgan le Fey?

I'll be thanking you not to liken little harmless winged creatures to the awesome idea of the fair folk! (Little fairies indeed?!)

A rather apt quote from Rudyard Kipling:

> Can you wonder that the People of the Hills don't care to be con-fused with that painty-winged, wand-waving, sugar-and-shake-your-head set of imposters? Butterfly wings, indeed!

I'd also request you to recall an ancient Celtic strategy of battle: "Fight and fight and run away—live to fight another day!" when considering dis-appearing into the hills or going underground, or to ground.

Did the Tuatha dé Danann take the most expedient and strategically successful initiative of removing themselves from the limelight to protect their knowledge and draíocht from being manipulated by those of the future?

Don't you think it plausible that so great a people possessed the ability to foresee what would happen? Wouldn't it be a cunning thing to do—to seemingly integrate with the conquerors while maintaining and passing on the lore and ways of the sacred?

And waiting?

Patiently?

Eventually disseminating around the world as time passed?

So . . . they're still here. And so is their knowledge. Accessing the anima of the draíocht is a matter of journeying into the Unseen-Real to enable you to experience that draíocht yourself.

The Four Cities (Thresholds)

Gorias: The Element of Air

The direction of the threshold into Gorias is east. The east represents the place of the "rising" sun and moon and star, and is therefore said to be the birthplace of these to earth; the sword is represented here, the symbol of merciful justice. The east—the element of air—represents the inspiration that comes from seemingly nowhere, and is the intuition that precedes creativity. It represents, essentially, intelligence—not the capacity to learn but rather the ability to understand what is learned.

The axiom "To Will" is associated with the element of air, and the tools of the Craft that represent it (within your ritual Circle and perhaps upon the journey) are the incense, athame, and sword.

The east is the place of dawn; the concept of birth and new beginnings; spring and its equinox.

Its Mythos: The Rite of Spring
Union of the Chosen One (He-Who-Runs-with-the-Stag)
with the Priestess of the Moon. His initiation as Priest/King.

The treasure sought and gained: inspiration and clear sight; knowledge gained from both information and practical application; knowledge; eagerness.

Finias: The Element of Fire

The direction of the threshold leading to Finias is south (in the Southern Hemisphere it is north). The staff dwells here, representing the craft of clear communication—all modes of oral or written expression and the tradition of the Seanachaì.

The axiom "To Dare" is associated with the element of fire, and the tools of the Craft that represent it (within your ritual Circle and perhaps/probably upon your journey) are the flame, the wand, and the staff.

The element of fire is midday, when the sun is at zenith; the fullness and prime of life; the actualization of an undertaking; summer and its solstice.

Its Mythos: The Rite of Summer
Sacrifice of the Sun King—
Transformation of One Form into Another—Cyclic Change.
The King is dead! All hail the once and future King!

This begins the waning of the year—the "dark" half—and the descent into the Underworld. The rule of the Holly King.

The treasure sought and gained: clear intent and the ability to act according to any circumstance; skill; courage and egoless authority; understanding gained as the result of knowledge; a sense of humor.

Murias: The Element of Water

The direction of the threshold into the Worlds of Mythos known as Murias will take you into the west; this represents the place of the setting sun, therefore, it is often called the "realm of the dying gods"; the Grail dwells here, the symbol of the Cauldron of Ceridwen (and all that it implies regarding how wisdom is sometimes gained).

The dark follows the setting of the sun.

The west is the place of the Island Remembered (also known as the Drowned Land), and represents deaths of outmoded thought and deed. To the individual it symbolizes human emotion.

Emotions can be difficult things to come to terms with. We can work with the discipline of many things, but emotion often tends to dominate us. It is necessary to reach deeply into the cauldron to tackle the "monsters" that can dwell therein.

The Cauldron of Plenty and Rebirth dwells in Murias. Wisdom, contemplation, reflection, resolution, endings preceding something else, and the power of letting go are the gifts and learning associated with it.

The axiom "To Keep Silent" is associated with the element of water, and the tools of the Craft that represent it within your ritual Circle are the chalice, the water, and the cauldron.

The element of water is sunset; the time of the solar year is autumn, specifically its equinox.

Its Mythos: The Rite of Autumn
The King lies sleeping upon the Sacred Isle
Guarded by the Ladies of the Lake—
The Wild Hunt begins.

It represents all Underworld journeys: to Tir na n'Ogh; the Isle of the Blessed; the Land of Elphame.

The treasure sought and gained: wisdom gleaned from knowledge and understanding; the art of resolution; a sense of both wonder and the absurd; scholarship; the way of the Wise Fool.

Falias: The Element of Earth

The direction you will take to pass the threshold into Falias is north (south in the Southern Hemisphere) and the element of earth: this represents pre-birth, hence rebirth in potential. The Lia Fáil dwells here— some say that the shield is a symbolic representation of the stone (and it's an apt representation).

Practicality, determination, the care of living things, which includes maintaining maximum health, the ability to cement ideas, inspirations, and so on, can only be achieved with a strong foundation. The element of earth also represents knowledge, both practical and philosophical/arcane.

The axiom "To Know" is associated with the element of earth, and the tools of the Craft that represent it in the ritual Circle are the pentacle, shield, and, sometimes, drum.

The time is midnight; the time of year is winter and its solstice.

Its Mythos: The Rite of Winter
Rebirth of the Sun God—the Boyhood and Training of a King.

It begins the "light" half of the Cycle of the Seasons. It is the time of the reign of the Oak King.

The treasure sought and gained: reflection; lucid dreaming; an ability to walk between the worlds and to come to know "the still point"; the art of letting go.

6 Wherefore Guards the Dragon!

The truthful answer is
"I am fifteen thousand million years old."

—Dr. Darryl Reanney

The Four Worlds are Many Things and Places

Annwn is likened to the Underworld, even the roots of the World Tree—it is an Otherworld where you can visit in ritual journeys and discover the past, the ancestors, and deep hidden knowledge; it is a place of self-challenge whereby your deepest fears can be met and faced, thereby giving access to your greatest courage. It is also the Land itself and all she has ever known, and to which we are forever connected.

Abred and *Gwynvyd* are likened to both the body and branches of the World Tree, the place of experience and life as we know it, and the realm of spirit within which all things are possible and where destiny, other than of a physical nature, is determined.

Ceugant is the sky from which the Tree breathes; it is boundless, infinite.

These last three are considered, also, as three interconnecting rings of life experience.

The symbolism is clear. To think only of the world that we perceive with our five senses is to deny access to what the ancients have always understood and the gift of their knowledge that they have passed to us.

Dragon lines are ley lines—potent, generative forces representing both the power of the land and sky as well as the energetic map of the body. They intersect and connect the earth to herself; are the tracks traveled by generation after generation; the unwritten migratory patterns of birds and animals; the Songlines or Imramma (mystical journeys) of ancient people living now through both blood and story; the well-trod route of traders and bards and pilgrims and roads connecting cities to other cities.

The dragon can represent both terrestrial and human qualities, for either one can at different times signify spiritual immortality, wisdom, re-embodiment, or regeneration.

Annwn [annooven]

The Underworld; the primal abyss; the place of pre-life; the unconscious wherein dwells all genetic memory, lost places, lost faces, unformed potential and the progression of all life. This is the place of the Dragon-Force, and the Dragon dwells at the mouth of the abyss and guards the untapped treasure reverently!

Annwn is the "Tail of the Dragon."

You enter this state at times of greatest testing—times of grief, times of trial, at the prospect of initiation, and during life-changes, including initiation into the priesthood.

It is eternal night, darkness of space, deepest of silences. We've all been there, or at least sensed that domain.

At times we all peer frighteningly into the void, but madness dwells there for the unwary, and we all tread the Extended Bridge of Knowledge before seeking the treasure.

Here (so say all legends known) goeth the Hero in search of a Grail, spending his time in the Savage Forest, removing obstacles and conflicting with beasts and demons on the journey of the quest.

Abred [abreth]

The earth. The place of day to day.

It is conscious awareness of the experiences, actions, responses, and reactions to everyday events; as such, you must be aware of the context of each event and the ripples (affecting the World Song) that your way of living are bound to create. Your choices are to be both claimed and owned and then responded to responsibly, as are the ramifications of those choices.

The witch's task is to learn to tread softly along the dragon lines of earth.

Abred is the "Body of the Dragon."

We all bring our own personal Mythos into play in every experience from having journeyed into Mythos, and the recognition of not only what we are doing but also how we are doing it is your concern here.

Abred is your physical "temple" or Nemeton, the sacred space in which you work draíocht, your dwelling (your hearth), your workplace, wherever you go, and whatever you do. It is First Seen-Real. It is interwoven with Annwn, with Gwynvyd, and thence with Ceugant, and if this is not forgotten it will make living a more profound and draíochta experience.

Gwynvyd [gooinvyth]

This is the state of all the interconnected Worlds of Mythos. It is both the Unseen-Real (your awareness of the many worlds) and the Second Seen-Real—the Mytho-Worlds themselves. Accessing Gwynvyd is gained by familiarity with the Otherworlds; by way of controlled visualization (the journey to) until you are within the Mythos (the experience of). The "muses" dwell there—they are another expression of Déithe, and it is they who inspire art, poetry, music, story, and vision (and one of them is driving me *really* intensely right now as I write!). The knowledge of Annwn and Abred are clear there; the ramifications of our draíocht are recorded there for all to see.

The Déithe meet with us in whatever form they choose in Gwynvyd. It's also like the Halls of Faerie that can trap the seeker by its glamour (meant in the older sense)—it all depends on why you go there.

Gwynvyd is the "Head of the Dragon."
The House of the Pendragon.

Ceugant [caigant]

This is the state of all draíochta, the wellspring from which the Déithe drink. It is the "oversoul" of time, energy, matter, and space. It truly is the Great Wheel, the Spiral Dance, and the place of all possibility. It cannot be understood by our minds (at this point in evolution, I might add) because no matter what we might understand, know, discover, or consider possible, there will always be more.

It *is* the Imramma, and as such it is forever immanent.

Ceugant is the "Dragon's Breath."

Or the whole of the Dragon—which brings to mind the axiom:

"The whole is always greater than the sum of its parts."

Ceugant is continually expanding, contracting, creating, and recreating, therefore how can we ever hope to know it? There is wonder in this thought! Mystery is, in its own right, power, and it is our inalienable right to seek that mystery; any who have crossed the threshold of Gwynvyd, even once, will understand wonder.

Ceugant is also the Forever Tree—we never go past the universe's next trick!

The Dragon is also ourselves
and the Dragon is the Earth
and the energetic field that encompasses the Earth
and the soul of Earth and all that is of Earth.

7

The Main Tools of a Practicing Witch

Pass the word and pass the lady, pass the plate to all who hunger.
Pass the wit of ancient wisdom, pass the cup of crimson wonder.

—Jethro Tull, "Cup of Wonder"

Care, contemplation, and "the law of attraction" are the most successful ways of "bonding" the things you will use in your ritual Circle. When in doubt, make your own. When this is not possible it is advisable to acquire what is *really* attractive to your sense of beauty and aesthetics.

I could be considered to possess a veritable arsenal of traditional weapons due to my love of martial arts, and these things *could* be considered as other than ritual things, except they're not—because all things are sacred, and more so when they are perceived as such by the practitioner of draíocht.

Housed in my sanctuary are four swords: one (very old) is used as the traditional double-bladed sword of the initiator and is never used outside of my ritual Circle, another broadsword is used in the traditional art associated with its use (and was hand-forged by an Australian blacksmith of some renown, as was the third), the third is a work of classic beauty forged in a style of ancient Mongolia, and the fourth is a traditional Ninja blade—fine, light, and my favored training blade. All are simple and unadorned.

I have Bo and Jo staves, of Tasmanian oak, bokken for training sessions with my friends, and both a recurve and a compound bow.

I don't use them in my ritual Circle, but my physical disciplines are also sacred arts.

The staff that I *do* use in my ritual Circle is an amazing thing. Many years ago I lived in a very old house in rural Victoria that had several elms growing outside my bedroom. One night, at the height of a raging thunderstorm, lightning struck one of the trees just outside my window where I stood watching the display, reveling (as one does) in the sheer magnificence of the spectacle. It struck one branch only. As the tempest receded I ran outside and brought the long, straight branch inside. It's black and tined. It's my ritual staff.

There are many stories of how one comes by one's ritual tools, and so it should be for you. Ultimately, it doesn't matter if you have none. They must be an extension of your own draíocht, but they must also have their own, otherwise they are pretensions.

The Basics

Athame

(Represents the Sword of Gorias.)

The black-hilted, double-edged dagger, known as an *athame,* has all the attributes of the sword and is used as an extension of one's will.

Although the traditional metal is iron, we know of those made of stainless steel, silver, bronze, as well as mixed metals of significance; some will set their blade with inlaid sigils, some have long, tapering blades, some are waving like a kris, some are sickled. Some have cross-pieces artistically and personally designed, perhaps set with certain stones. The hilts I have seen defy limitation, except in the mind of the witch; some are carved from ebony in the likeness of the body of a woman, with a hand-carved, silver capital; some are willow spirals, and others are bound in red-belly black snakeskin. They are rowan or oak, or velvet entwined in silken braid. All are unique and either hand-done or hand-finished. My own is a traditional leaf-shaped, pattern-welded blade (it's the one with the rowan-wood hilt bound in red-belly black snakeskin entwined with silken braid!).

A sword is not necessary, and should not replace the energy you have imbued into your athame.

Your athame, when procured, is taken into your Circle and consecrated. It is never left lying about. It is never used outside the domain of your Circle. It is never used to draw blood. It is a tool of invocation and consecration.

Wand and Staff

(Represents the Spear of Finias.)

The wand has all the attributes of the staff (you can have a staff as well). It represents the communication of the *intent* of the ritual (as well as the communication itself), which is most important, as many workings are not conducive to the spoken word, and the wand is used to convey messages between you and Déithe when you don't want to "speak."

It also represents the Lord of the Forest (as does the tined staff).

When it is cut for shaping, the wand is traditionally measured from elbow to the tip of your middle finger. It's also important to realize that you cannot cut a living branch for the purpose of making your wand and/or staff. My wand is of rowan twigs, taken from the dead branch of a living tree, bound together with plaited thread and sealed at each end with red sealing-wax. It is ornamented with small bronze bells, plaits of my own hair, and a raven's feathers.

The wand can be left plain, oiled, or polished with beeswax; it can be painted, carved, hung with fetishes of your totems, set with sigils of silver and gold; it can have a crystal as a capital, be hollowed out and filled with ground semi-precious stones, or you can simply have your name written in pen and ink down its length.

When you've prepared your wand (and/or your staff), you take it into your Circle and consecrate it, then wrap it in cloth or leather. It is never left lying around where it could be handled by others.

Chalice

(Represents the Cauldron of Murias.)

The chalice (also called the cup) represents the Grail in your Circle (there is usually a cauldron also). It is used to consecrate the wine; it can also be used for scrying, and as such it is also a mirror.

The chalice is the Grail remembered, the cornucopia, symbol of the fertilizing power of the Waters of Life, and also the womb.

Within your Circle it represents Déithe in her fecund and life-giving capacity, and as such it represents love and will be upon your altar as a representative of the Mórrigan and her priestess (if not in the flesh, most assuredly in spirit).

It's mostly silver or silver-plated, as this is the metal of the moon (as gold is the metal of the sun).

However hard you try it is most difficult to have a chalice made, and for this reason I suggest that you buy it—do not quibble over cost, though, if it is what you want.

Pentacle

(Represents the Lia Fáil.)

The pentacle represents the shield in your Circle (sometimes a drum/bodhrán is used to summon the elementals of earth). It's used in all acts of invocation, especially relating to the elements, elementals, threshold-guardians. It represents the earth herself. It is used specifically at all banishings, house blessings, consecrations, bindings, and protections. Its summoning powers, when properly prepared, lend surcease to physical and material hindrance.

The traditional pentacle is a copper disc; this is usually about fifteen centimeters in diameter and about two centimeters in thickness. The disc is hand-carved with the sigils of your Craft, the main theme being the pentagram. It is then buried in the path of the waxing moon from new to full (during which time, all going well, it should be turning from red-brown to green, the color of Venus), then it is dug up and consecrated in your Circle.

Alternatives to copper have been highly polished wood, clay, stone, and, occasionally, wax. I have not known of any other materials being used, as I feel that they would be contrary to the element of earth.

The traditional bodhrán or one of the easily available "shaman" drums are exceptionally good at inducing trance and ecstasy—a practical pre-journey state to be in, as the rhythm can be ridden like the horse.

The pentacle, likewise, is not used outside of a ritual Circle, although the drum most often is.

Part 3

Ritual

8   Theory and Practice

*And I would stand / if the night blackened with a coming storm /
beneath some rock, listening to notes that are / the ghostly language of the
ancient earth, / or make their dim abode in distant winds. /
Thence did I drink the visionary power.*

—William Wordsworth, *The Prelude*

Circle, Sanctuary, Nemeton, Grove

A Circle is cast before each rite to form a temporary protection, which is resolved once the rite is done.

A sanctuary is an indoor place that is like a temple—it is not used as a place-in-common with others.

A grove is an outdoor sanctuary, or nemeton.

Set up the place where the ritual is to be worked. The key to preparation is simple—perfection. You should eat nothing for a few hours prior to performing the ritual.

Preparation

If you are working the ritual indoors you'll probably have acquired a trunk or box, a large flat stone, or a table of some kind (if you're using a table, it's preferable, again, that it be used for this purpose to the exclusion of other things) to serve as your altar.

Outdoors is easy; the whole thing's one big altar unless you choose otherwise.

Upon the altar you'll have a censer (thurible or incense burner—other names for the same thing), an altar-flame (candle or other), your pentacle, athame, chalice, wand, dishes for salt and water, your Book of Shadows opened at the ritual (in case you haven't learned the ritual yet), and anything else that has been consecrated or that you consider sacred. You will also need to remember your grimoire for the recording of anything significant, and a pen with which to write.

Reive (clean and clear in a focused manner) the area.

You will need four candles (or lanterns for outdoors), each in its own candlestick, for lighting the threshold of each element. These are set within the boundary of the Circle at the four quadrants of a compass.

If your outdoor sanctuary is going to be used consistently, place four stones or specially prepared staves at these quadrants (set, preferably, at sunrise on the Winter Solstice).

Your altar is set to the north in the northern lands (south in the Southern Hemisphere), the place of earth where all potential dwells. It symbolizes the *foundation* of your Craft and it is never ready until the flame upon it is alight, which represents the light that dwells within all sacred environments and lights your way between the worlds.

Before beginning the ritual you are to bathe (or shower) with the express purpose of cleansing away all that is of no significance to the rite.

Prepare a jar of blended oils, which will be consecrated for preparation of your body. It is best to use a base of either olive or sweet-almond oil (three-quarters of a jar), and add to it the essential oils that you are most attracted to, or that you feel represent you. This jar of oil is kept for your personal use only.

After the bath (to which it is good to add a little salt and a drop of oil) you are to oil your body and go to the prepared place. Work naked or robed (depending on how you are most comfortable).

Light the altar-flame as well as the incense, and ground and center yourself. Use either four-fold breathing or a soft humming chant to focus and stabilize yourself.

Through the technique of visualization you'll build an energy grid around the sanctuary or grove until it forms a domelike spiral of interconnecting ley lines, spinning, always spinning in the direction of the sun (counterclockwise in the southern hemisphere, clockwise in the northern—sunwise being called "deosil").

When the image is substantial and fixed you will walk the Circle of the ritual place summoning the Déithe to aid and protect the space for the period of your ritual. It's *much* better to use words that are appropriate to you rather than read them by rote without any thought of what you say, as everything that is done within a ritual is to be very real and intentional.

(You'll continue to focus on the spiral of ley lines that comprise your Circle for the whole of the ritual.)

Invoking Earth's Guardian

Light the candle at Gate of Earth and summon the guardian:

> *Come ye, of the northern (southern) winds,*
> *Place of storms and deepest night,*
> *Place of silence most profound.*
> *Acknowledge and guard this Circle,*
> *Summoned by the names of N . . . (name the Déithe, Lady, and Lord).*
> *Open for me the Gate of Earth!*

Draw, with your hand, the invoking pentagram of Earth:

Invoking pentagram of Earth.

See a Gate of enormous proportions, entwined with ivy and morning glory. Your pentagram acts as a sign to those that guard the Gate that you are aware and prepared, and so they will open it toward you.

The scene behind the Gate is of vast primordial forests seen from within their depths. The guardian will come through the forest toward you, either alone or attended by the elementals of Earth and any or many of her creatures.

The guardian will mirror your pentagram and will flood your Circle with deep green light.

Invoking Air's Guardian

You then walk toward the east, light the candle, and summon the guardian:

> *Come ye, of the East winds,*
> *Place of Sunrise and the rise of Moon,*
> *Place of inspiration.*
> *Acknowledge and guard this Circle,*
> *Summoned in the names of N . . . (name the Déithe, Lady, and Lord).*
> *Open for me the Gate of Air!*

Draw, with your hand, the invoking pentagram of Air:

Invoking pentagram of Air.

See a Gate of enormous proportions, made of silver and shimmering with light. Your pentagram acts as a sign to those who guard the Gate that you are aware and prepared, and so it is opened.

The scene behind the Gate is as though you stood upon the highest mountain of the world and could see as far as forever. There are swiftly flying clouds, and birds flying around and beneath where you stand. The guardian comes toward you, dipping and riding the currents and tides, either alone or attended by the hosts of the elementals of Air.

The guardian mirrors your pentagram and floods your Circle with the golden-yellow light of dawn.

Invoking Fire's Guardian

You move to the south (north in the Southern Hemisphere), Gate of Fire, and light the candle and summon the guardian:

Come ye, of the southern (northern) winds,
Place of the highest Sun,
Place of Creation manifest.
Acknowledge and guard this Place,
Summoned in the names of the N . . . (name the Déithe, Lady, and Lord).
Open for me the Gate of Fire!

Draw, with your hand, the invoking pentagram of Fire:

Invoking pentagram of Fire.

See before you a Gate of massive proportions made of gold. Your penta-gram acts as a sign to the guardian that you are aware and prepared, and so the Gate will open.

The scene behind the Gate is of a volcano as it is viewed from its lip, of suns and stars revolving in a dance about each other.

The guardian comes toward you from the heart of the volcano, either alone or attended by the elementals of fire, and will mirror your penta-gram and flood your Circle with fiery-red light.

Invoking Water's Guardian

Lastly, you go to the west and light the candle and summon the guardian:

> *Come ye, of the West winds,*
> *Place of the setting Sun,*
> *Home of the Island Remembered,*
> *Place of Wisdom.*
> *Acknowledge and guard this Circle,*
> *Summoned in the names of N . . . (name the Déithe, Lady, and Lord).*
> *Open for me the Gate of Water!*

Draw, with your hand, the invoking pentagram of Water:

Invoking pentagram of Water.

See the massive Gate, the metal a deep aqua-blue, the wavelets of a vast ocean lapping at its base from the other side.

Your pentagram informs the guardian that you are aware and prepared, and so the Gate opens toward you. Just behind the Gate are dark boulders that lead to the sea. There are creatures of the oceans to be seen in all directions—whales and dolphins; great, flat stingray; octopus; and there is movement, arrow-shaped, as great schools of fish travel their patterns.

The guardian comes toward you out of the depths, either alone or attended by the elementals of water. The guardian will mirror your pentagram and flood your Circle with deep-blue light.

Return to your altar and prepare for the consecration of your ritual things.

Consecration

Your first consideration is your athame. This tool is the witch's representation of will and intent, and it acts as an extension of you. It is always double-edged, symbolizing compassion and severity in balance.

To consecrate your athame you will need to have the following in your Circle with you: wine, chalice, salt and water (and the containers to hold the latter), some essential oil (musk and jasmine are easily obtainable, and mixed together they symbolize the Déithe of Lady and Lord), a white candle, and your incense.

These things, along with your athame, are placed on your altar while the preparations for the ritual take place (casting the Circle, summoning the guardians).

Light the special white candle and raise your athame, blade pointed up, then call the names of the Déithe (Lady and Lord) to aid you with the draíocht, and ask that they bless the athame. Draw the invoking pentagrams of Earth, Air, Fire, and Water over it.

I invoke the draíocht of Earth, Sky, and Sea,
And thus invoked I link myself to thee!

Then hold the athame against your body, point down, and watch as light from the ley lines that form your Circle web out to entwine around both you and your athame. This energy passes through the blade and thence into your own body, where it will be seen as travelling in spirals through you and back out through the blade, leaving and merging with the Circle again.

Take up your athame and draw the sign of the invoking pentagram of Spirit (the same as the pentagram of Earth, on page 43, except that the focus is from the topmost point to the subsequent four other points: "From Spirit, to Earth, to Air, to Fire, to Water") over the salt and say:

Blessings be upon thee.

Draw the sign of the pentagram of Spirit over the water and say:

Blessings be upon thee.

Add the salt to the water, and draw the sign of the pentagram of Spirit upon your forehead with it, saying:

Hail to thee N . . . (name the Déithe, Lady, and Lord),
I ask your blessings with the draíocht.

Work the salt and water into the athame, both blade and hilt.

Take the oil and draw the pentagram of spirit over it, saying:

I consecrate thee, and fill thee with draíocht.
I bid thee, aid me in my task!

Work the oil into your athame, blade, and hilt.

Take the chalice of wine and draw the pentagram of Spirit over it, saying:

Thou art blessed, Fruit of the Lord of the Earth!

Work the wine into your athame, blade, and hilt.

Now take the athame and pass it through the flame at the Gate of Fire, saying:

The draíocht of Fire infuse my blade.

Pass it through the water and salt, saying:

The draíocht of Water infuse my blade.

Pass it through the incense, saying:

The draíocht of Air infuse my blade.

Then place the athame, blade down, upon the ground, saying:

The draíocht of Earth infuse my blade.

Place your athame against your chest and close your eyes, concentrating all of your love into it.

Allow enough time to be absolutely certain that your objective has been met, then say:

Shh, be at peace now—we are at one with Déithe.

Kiss your newly consecrated athame on both blade and hilt, and return it to your altar.

The pattern for consecrations generally follows this format, but in the future the pentagrams (all of them) of summoning will be done with your athame in hand. Prior to ritual, and after, the blade of your athame is to be gently rubbed with a magnet to ensure its draíocht is maintained.

Any other intention you wish to pursue is undertaken while still in the Circle.

Concluding Invocations

When you are done, you are to honor the guardians through the act of farewell.

Earth

Go to the Gate of Earth. The guardian is standing sentinel at the open Gate. Raise your arms, athame in your right hand, and say:

I am allied to the Déithe of Earth.
Wherever they have need of me there shall I be.
I give honor where it is due—great powers of Earth I salute you!

Draw the banishing pentagram of Earth with your athame, and watch as it disappears:

Banishing pentagram of Earth.

The guardian acknowledges your pentagram and closes the Gate. Extinguish the candle to the north (south in the Southern Hemisphere).

Air

Proceed to the Gate of Air. The guardian is standing sentinel at the open Gate. Raise your arms, athame in your right hand, and say:

> *I am allied to the Déithe of Air.*
> *Wherever they may have need of me, there will I be.*
> *I give honor where it is due. Great powers of Air I salute you!*

Draw the banishing pentagram of Air with your athame:

Banishing pentagram of Air.

The guardian acknowledges your pentagram and closes the Gate. Extinguish the candle to the east.

Fire

Go to the Gate of Fire. See the guardian standing sentinel at the open Gate. Raise your arms, athame in your right hand, and say:

> *I am allied to the Déithe of Fire.*
> *Wherever they may have need of me, there shall I be.*
> *I give honor where it is due. Great Powers of Fire I salute you!*

Draw the banishing pentagram of Fire with your athame:

Banishing pentagram of Fire.

The guardian will acknowledge your pentagram and close the Gate. Extinguish the candle to the south (north in the Southern Hemisphere).

Water

At the Gate of Water you see the guardian standing sentinel. Raise your arms, athame in your right hand, and say:

I am allied to the Déithe of Water.
Wherever they may have need of me, there shall I be.
I give honor where it is due. Great powers of Water I salute you!

Draw the banishing pentagram of Water with your athame:

Banishing pentagram of Water.

The guardian acknowledges your pentagram and closes the Gate. Extinguish the candle to the west.

To withdraw the Circle you walk against the Sun (clockwise, or "widdershins," in the Southern Hemisphere, counterclockwise in the Northern), drawing energy of the spiral of ley lines into the blade of your athame as you do so. When it is done you will place your athame blade into the earth, where it is absorbed.

When it's all done, you will softly say:

The rite is done, by Earth, by Sky, by Sea.

Then, prior to earthing yourself (see below), you will record in your grimoire anything of importance.

Earthing

The process of grounding or earthing is imperative after working within your Circle.

First, you are to rub your body down the arms, then flick the energy off your hands; rub down your legs, then flick the energy off your hands; rub down your torso and as much of your back as you can reach, then flick the energy off your hands; rub over your face and head, then flick the energy off your hands.

Second, you are to go and either drink down a full glass of water or eat some food (remember, you would not have done so for about three hours prior to the ritual).

Third, put away all of your ritual things.

Don't get drawn into day-to-day conversation afterward if you can help it—it'll just annoy you.

9 Notes on the Four Elements

Many words are spoken when there's nothing to say
They fall upon the ears of those who don't know the way
To read between the lines, that lead between the lines . . .

—Alan Parson's Project, "The Eagle Will Rise Again"

This is merely a ground plan of each of the elements. Learn them and expand upon them through personalized understanding as you go. Once you have become familiar with the associations you can proceed to the ritual invocations and familiarizations of the Déithe of each Gate, remembering to earth yourself after each working.

Every ritual that you do will have an effect on your life—if you can keep that in mind throughout, then you will be careful as to what you invoke (remember the Law of Congruity: cause and effect).

The Earth Deithe

Environmental
All solid matter, from the earth herself to the materials of both organic and inorganic matter, right down to the cellular level of all living things.

Personal Qualities (These are Generalizations)
In balance: the nature of your material body is maintained at its maximum potential (less for the ego of having a "beautiful" body as for the ability

to perpetuate survival at its optimum); your ability to order your financial situation so that you do not starve to death; your ability to organize; your ability to manifest those things in your life that can otherwise remain only at inspiration point; all training methods that allow free expression of who you are (for example, learning the ABCs so that you can read and write; learning about color, space, and so on; but if you wish to paint, for instance, you will need a physical training regime).

Out of balance: the opposite of all the above.

Some Traditional Associations

It is represented in the direction of *north* in the Northern Hemisphere (south in the Southern Hemisphere); the archangelic force is named Uriel; the elemental king is named Ghobb; the elementals are known as Gnomes; in Qabbalah, earth represents the World of Assiah; the time of day ruling this element is midnight; the time of the solar year is Winter Solstice; the ritual tool is the pentacle; on the Otherworld isle known as Avalon, the Sacred Regalia is represented as the shield and the stone.

The Air Deíthe

Environmental

Oxygen; all gasses; atmospheric pressure; aerial currents, and the winds that accompany them; the spaces between places.

Personal Qualities (These are Generalizations)

In balance: a "healthy" curiosity/intellect; inspiration; the ability to learn; the ability to be "open" to the draíocht; the essence of both honor and cooperation; and the *quality* of speech.

Out of balance: the opposite of all the above.

Some Traditional Associations

The direction is *east;* the archangelic force is named Raphael; the elemental king is named Paralda; the elementals are known as Sylphs; in the

Qabbalah, air represents the World of Yetzirah; the time of day ruling this element is dawn; the time of the solar year is the Spring Equinox; the ritual tool is the athame; on the Otherworld isle known as Avalon, the Sacred Regalia is the sword Excalibur.

The Fire Deithe

Environmental

Volcanic activity; the sun; lightning; electricity (in all its forms); the ion; all forms of flame; the heat that sustains life in the bodies of all living creatures (the metabolic function).

Personal Qualities (These are Generalizations)

In balance: spontaneity; excitement; sexual excitement; all creativity; the ability to manifest ideas into actions by the essence of personal "drive"; the ability to inspire others through the spoken or the written word; constructive anger.

Out of balance: apathy; all forms of violence; sloth; jealousy; spite.

Some Traditional Associations

The direction is *south* in the Northern Hemisphere (north in the Southern Hemisphere); the archangelic force is named Michael; the elemental king is named Djinn; the elementals are known as Salamanders; in the Qabbalah, fire is known as the World of Atziluth; the time of day is midday; the time of the solar year is the Summer Solstice; the ritual tool is the wand and staff; on the Otherworld isle of Avalon, the Sacred Regalia is the spear.

The Water Deithe

Environmental

All liquids; the fluid parts of all living bodies; rain; dew; sap; oceans; rivers; subterranean waterways and lakes; mists and fog; clouds.

Personal Qualities (These are Generalizations)

In balance: love; compassion; awareness; cooperation; instinct; the trans-
mutation of experience and learning into wisdom; psychic ability.

Out of balance: the opposite of all the above, but we will include cynicism,
sarcasm, alcoholism, and all addictions including obsessions; and spiritual naivete (that is, herd, or mob, mentality).

Some Traditional Associations

The direction is *west;* the archangelic force is named Gabriel; the elemental king is named Nixsa; the elementals are Undines; in Qabbalah, water
represents the World of Briah; the time of day is sunset; the time of the
solar year is Autumn Equinox; the ritual tool is the chalice and the cauldron; on the Otherworld known as Avalon, the Sacred Regalia is the
Grail.

This is all about familiarizing yourself with the draíocht (whether traditional or spontaneous) so that the flow is "in the body" rather than merely
theoretical.

Through personal understanding—through the rituals—through
alliance with the Déithe of the worlds of the four elements, and the inhab-
itants therein, you merge with Imramma and your part in its continuum.

When you summon the guardians within these rituals, it's advanta-
geous to realize the following: they, unlike the elementals that attend
them, *do* understand; they *do* react. They are Déithe with full intelligence
of the patterns, and they can be either allies or enemies, depending on
your intent; they have had much to deal with since the advent of our
industrial and technological revolutions, and they are not amused by
those who seek self-glory at their expense, or the expense of the domin-
ions that they guard.

Progressing the Relationship with the Guardians and their Worlds

When seeking to journey any of the elemental worlds exclusively—to acclimatize yourself to them—you only require the casting of your Circle and the invoking of the particular guardian. You can spend your entire ritual exploring each world.

At the conclusion of each working, after returning to your Circle in the Seen-Real, farewell the Déithe, open the Circle with your athame, and earth the energy to end the rite.

Part 4

The Faces of God

10 Visualizations and Invocations

*Only . . . with the closing of the lips of the last mortal who
preserved his tradition can the life of a god be truly said to end.*

—Charles Squire, *Celtic Myths and Legends*

Here we begin, by breaking into segments, the different pantheons associated with draíocht and witchcraft: the Déithe that witches find both familiar and comfortable. Progress and expand your own research in your own time, as this book is meant mainly for practical training and it is preferable that you follow through on theory as life allows.

You will find it beneficial to seek out the myths and legends of Greek, Roman, or Norse traditions, the Finno-Ugric traditions, the Egyptian, Babylonian, Sumerian, and Hebrew understandings of what constitutes "sacred" and "magic," those of both North and South America, and the Aboriginal legends of the Dreamtime, Shamanic, and Druidic traditions. Have a good look at Qabbalah. In the Gnostic and the early Christian traditions you will find threads that lead into Deep-Time and the sacredness of other cultures' traditions. They will all show you that there is little or nothing new, and if you seek deeply enough you will most certainly find that the core of all of them is fundamentally the same; there is also much interest in the early Eastern traditions, especially tantra.

There are several persona of Déithe for you to come to know through invocation.

The first step is to understand, intellectually, the deeper significance of each, and then come to understand, emotionally, which of them, specifically, is aligned with your own desires, spirit, aspirations, and, of course, your personality.

The second step is to invoke that persona as your "mentor," as the Déithe thus invoked can become a benefactor that will seek to manifest through you, and, because this persona is initially most comfortable for you, it is, again, your line of least resistance (like attracts like).

And finally, you will work with the others simply because no one and nothing living is one-dimensional, or lacking in paradox.

You'll invoke these Déithe singularly, to fully comprehend what they mean to you personally, as opposed to generally. Each is given an individuality within the Worlds of Mythos through which you will travel—this is by no means set in stone—I present them as they have appeared to me (and to others).

You'll work at deepening your knowledge of draíocht through contemplation, visualization, inspiration, and invocation, by knowing each of the Déithe, by allowing them to "touch" you. When this has been achieved you will be ready to work the rituals.

The Persona of Solar/Earth Deíthe

Lugh [loo]

He is Lord of the Shining Light. His nature is truth. He is divine justice, excellent intention, honor, and the protector of that which is honorable.

He represents the Champion of the Mórrigan, as the spear of light to humanity, and as such he represents the projection of your highest aspirations into your day-to-day life, and the (unattached) outcomes; he is the representation of your initiation more than you as a "mere" mortal.

He is master of all crafts and physical training.

As with most of the Déithe of the Celtic pantheon, he represents the fullness of life (including both love and the betrayal of love) and the transition of life, death, and rebirth. His symbol (when seen) is the spear. The golden eagle is the totem of his death.

He is seen as a shining scholar/warrior, accompanied, always, by two ravens. He holds his spear, point down, before him.

His other names are Belucadros and Mabon.

Artu [artoo]

Also known as Arthur/Ardrì—high king/pendragon—he symbolizes the sun made manifest as a man. He can be equated with all the "sacrificed gods" (wheat and corn and oats and barley, lamb and bull and stag). He is the brother, lover, and son of the Mórrigan, known to Artu by other names.

He is represented in all the legends of Avalon as symbolizing the seasons of earth, spirit, and "man," consecutively. He is the hope of the people for knowledge and manifest justice, as well as equality through unselfish love. He is one aspect of the Stag-King, champion of the people, whoever they may be, when oppression and hopelessness are the games played upon them by offending regimes.

He is the Great King, the Lord of Life and Death, the Initiated (anointed) One. His symbol is the sword; his totem is the dragon, and oft-times also the bear and the stag (in fact, all of these totems [sacred animals] are appropriate here).

He is seen dressed in crimson, and is crowned with a simple tri-pronged circlet of gold, a torque of gold around his throat with shapes of serpent or dragon entwined within it representing the wisdom of cyclic change. His symbols are tattooed onto the cheeks of his face—on the left cheek is the tattoo of a crow/raven (the Mórrigan), and on the right cheek is the tattoo of a dragon (the symbol of the Ardrì—high king). He holds a sword.

He is the Anointed One—Man, King, and God. He is the symbol of the fullness of life, waxing and waning with the seasons of sun, sky, and seed, but he cannot exist in the Seen-Real of the day to day unless through the love and embodiment of his solar/earth priests.

As the dead and dying king he dwells in the Mists of the Holy Isle-Outside-of-Time (Gwynvyd) until he is invoked into manifestation.

His other names are Dagda [dahada] (the Good God), In Daghdha, and also Mabon.

Bel [bell]

He is also the symbol of the sun, but has no true manifest form; he is the symbol of the energy of the solar force. As such, invocation and meditation of him means meditation on the symbol of the sun or solar wheel itself.

The Fire Festival of Beltane is named for him.

His other names are Belenos and Beli.

Astrologically, he represents the sun.

Hu [hyoo]

He is the God of the Grain—the Harvest Lord—the God of Life, inspiration, growth, the seed. As such, he is also the Bearer of the Seeds of Tomorrow.

He is Hu Gadarn, for your studies; he is consort to the Earth Mother and is symbolic of the Rites of Passage associated with the solar wheel, especially the solstices and equinoxes. He is Déithe of fecundity, of joy, of giving and the sharing of the earth's bounty.

You'll see him dressed in green, with a red cloak and a many-pronged crown of gold; his hair is the color of ripe grain.

He is joyous, laughing. He is the epitome of fertility, in both thought and deed.

His other names are Bres and Sucellus. (He can be equated with Dionysis and Bacchus, and also, due to his cyclic associations with the seasons, with Osiris.)

Lancelet [lanselet]

Also known as Lancelet du Lac, he is the symbol of the seeker who has not yet found his way to the Grail. He symbolizes the one who sacrifices "acceptable" existence due to his deep love of an ideal. He is torn between his desire to fight for the cause of freedom and self-determination (in conjunction with his beloved Arthur) and his desire for personal love. His love, both personal and idealistic, is the Grail herself (or oneness with the Wellspring), his symbol.

The invocation of Lancelet does not in any way reflect that you will be denied physical/personal love, but that you will sacrifice "normal" (the common paradigm) male sexual behavior and, unlike the noninitiated man, you will view physical loving and the sexual act itself as an act of "the sacred" to be shared with the Lady through her women—he therefore takes from the sex act the role of rutting or fornication and transforms it into a passionate act of love. He does not do this only by way of sex, but by way of love of earth.

He is not the "thinking" philosopher, but the "doing" philosophy.

He appears dressed in the deep red/orange of sunset, and bears a cup (grail) outheld to you. His eyes hold both wonder and a touch of some past madness.

Although he is most definitely a warrior Déithe, his motives are passive, passionate, and defensive, rather than active, analytical, and confrontative.

Other names that he is most certainly known by are Oengus/Aengus.

Merlin

Merlin (the Younger and the Elder; considered separately in context) has two faces. You are to invoke him with that awareness, as he may choose to appear with either the younger or the older.

He is the Déithe of learning; master of draíocht, of mystery, of the ways of making, changing, and shapeshifting; of that which is both ancient and intelligent.

Of story and legend he is famed—a *seanachaí* [shan-ukh-ee] (storyteller); a bard and a trickster. There is not one among us who has not yearned to know him and to know what he knows, for he is the epitome of the arcane and the sage—men's magic (of the sea, he is also the counterpart of the great and legendary Morgan le Fey).

He is, first, the messenger of the other Déithe—those who dwell in Caer Ceugant, and is also the messenger of the Mórrigan and the Herald of the Future. Do not seek him as his ancient self only, as he can be as bright and shining as either Lugh or Artu, but after another fashion. He also represents the Upholder-of-the-Law (tradition), but he is not a warrior god. He carries a (the) book and a (the) harp; the book symbolizes knowledge and truth through experience, and the harp is the music of life and the purveyor of enchantment.

He is invoked in either his aspect of master of draíocht (as is Math), or his aspect of truthsayer, enchanter, and prophet; in either of these aspects he may appear either young or old.

The persona of Merlin the Younger (akin to Taliesin) is cowled and robed in a cloak the color of mist or early morning light. The book will be in his right hand, and the harp in his left. He may even let you look into the book!

As Merlin the Elder he also represents time, in which case he will be cowled and robed in black and will carry a scythe in his left hand and the book in his right. When invoking this master of draíocht you must remember that he has a geas, as does everyone, and it is this: he will be swayed by his dogmatic belief in tradition to the point where he will not bend, and as time's natural path is change, he is undone by Nimuë, who represents "tomorrow."

There is no figure that is quite like Merlin.

No other has had as profound an impact on our concept of the druid/wizard/witch/enchanter/sorcerer.

His other name is Myrddin. He is likened to Chronos (as is Bran), Charon, Hermes, and Math.

Cernunnos [Kernoonos]

Also known as Cerne or Karnayna, he is our Great Lord of the Untamed, Lord of Beasts, the wild draíocht of woods, forests, mountains, deep valleys, and particularly of animals (including the animal-self). He is the primal in you, and as such he has been greatly feared in "civilized" consciousness (early Christians, and even today's, have turned him around so as to appear evil, which he most definitely is not).

Women yearn for him in their dreams (and even in their waking states if they fear not their own wildness). He is raw force. He is also savagery and tenderness (see appendix C: "To Ride the Tiger").

He is invoked at risk. "Why?" you may ask. Because most men have succeeded in burying him and his essence within the depths of their unconscious out of fear that the Christian patriarchs were right and that he is really their devil-in-drag (complete with horns and tail)!

Therefore, be aware when you invoke him that his "replica," distorted and corrupted to resemble something that Cernunnos is *not,* has been responsible for all manner of rape and other unacceptable sexual dynamics.

Cernunnos, Lord of the Wild, has been repressed and misrepresented for a very long time.

He is invoked, through ritual, in matters pertinent to the wild places when it is necessary to prevent destruction of his natural domain—and this is to assist him and the Earth Mother in their defense against those who would rob them blind!

He is also invoked to protect his witches from danger directly associated with those adverse to our working draíocht.

However, invoke him you will, as part of your training, but you must earth yourself well when you are done.

Cernunnos is known as "the God of the Witches," and for very clear reasons: he is the personification of the four elements, and when invoked he will appear as an enormous, physically powerful Man/God—his nakedness is his mantle; the horns of the Great Stag grow from his forehead and a gold torque surrounds his powerful throat. He is both beautiful and awe-full, and he will impart that proud, free, wild energy to you.

He has been mixed up, over time, with Herne the Hunter, but they are not the same persona of Déithe—Herne being Forest Lord and leader of the Wild Hunt (more on this later).

Gwydion [gooidion]

He is the inheritance of Math, Lord of the Underworld. He is a Master of Vision, and as such will also be a teacher to you.

He is invoked to develop personal power and the dignity, without affectation, that is the hallmark of a well-trained witch. It is the quality of your attitude—you are not prim, or conservative, or completely tame. When you invoke him you invoke the deep teachings relative to the draíocht.

He is associated with two of the goddesses—known as Rhiannon and Arianhrod (legend has it that he joined with Arianhrod, who was his "sister," to produce the awe-inspiring Lugh).

When you enter Mythos you'll see him: dressed in leather and furs with a cloak about his shoulders the colors of which comprise russet (autumn) and deep, rich violets; you can almost smell his rich, loamy presence. Joining the cloak at the neck is the brooch of a raven wrought of heavy silver—he is essentially Déithe of the Underworld (Annwn).

He bears a sword, which he keeps in a silver scabbard, symbolic of the fact that he is the Champion of the Mórrigan.

He wears a headdress of crow feathers upon his head like a crown. His stance is straight and strong. He is not cocky; he's proud; not vain, but dignified.

Nothing attacks him. He represents the "adept."

He's the "brother" Déithe of Artu, Gwyn ap Nudd, Herne, and Merlin.

Manannan

Déithe of the Sea (as such, he represents your deep-mind). He is approached when you have irrational fears or unresolved problems. He symbolizes primordial beginnings and represents all that dwells beneath the surface of the supposed civilized veneer of people.

He is also the essence of the shapeshifter (as are many of the Déithe) and imparts the gift of invisibility—to be seen, but not seen. He bestows the ability to "see" that which cannot be seen, and as such he is also associated with scrying in all its aspects, and the Unseen-Real known as Gwynvyd.

He protects your "soul-search."

He appears as a nebulous, mist-moving, not-quite-there Déithe of the Sea. He appears differently each time he is invoked, but the tinge of green about him and the unmistakable smell of brine will accompany him at each working. There's definitely an aspect of the trickster about him (Robin Goodfellow).

It is advised that you invoke his wisdom and strategy when preparing for any form of initiation, as he will assist you to "sneak up" on those fears and phantasms that inhabit your subconscious that can block the heights (or depths) of your draíocht.

He is the essence of changeability.

Diancecht [dian-ket]

He is the Déithe of healing. He is associated with wells, and the Cauldron of Ceridwen. His symbols are both the mortar and the pestle.

There is no set description of him, but he is invoked in all matters pertaining to healing. He is the Déithe of the herb and the natural healing agents that come to us from the wild, as well as being the representative of draíochta healing.

He will, however, usually appear in a forest grove or a high-cliff cave with a fire and a cauldron, surrounded with the wildcrafted herbs and experiments of his art.

Other names that can be associated with him are Bile and Nodens.

Taliesin [tal-i-essin]

> I have been in many shapes before I attained a congenial form. I have been a narrow blade of a sword; I have been a drop in the air; I have been a shining star; I have been a word in a book; I have been a book in the beginning; I have been a light in a lantern a year and a half; I have been a bridge passing over three-score rivers; I have journeyed as an eagle; I have been a boat on the sea; I have been a director in battle; I have been a sword in the hand; I have been a shield in fight; I have been a string of a harp; I have been enchanted for a year in foam of water. There is nothing in which I have not been.
>
> —From *The Book of Taliesin*

He is the Déithe of "projected knowledge." He is, literally, the force behind the spoken word. While keeping alive within our memory the instinctive knowledge that has been inherited from the past through discipline and seeking, he also projects that knowledge into the future—therefore, he could, today, be considered as the wisdom behind technology (in difference to mere technology itself).

He is as shamanic as the other Déithe insofar as he represents the essence of them all, along with the curious ability to transform inspiration into actuality; thus he is the very heart alchemy.

He can be seen, when invoked, surrounded with a glowing "mist" of faintly blue light. He stands before an altar upon which rest all the ritual tools that lay upon your own. He is neither "inside" nor "outside," as he dwells upon the border of all things (there is, however, no book, as he also represents skill of memory).

He always stands upon the threshold between today and tomorrow, thus we have found it easiest to invoke him at the hours between sunset and night.

He is also known as Ogmios/Ogma and Merlin the Younger.

Math

He is the Déithe of the Underworld—the benevolent, just, and beneficent Déithe of the Between-World (Annwn). In *Magic Arts in Celtic Britain,* Lewis Spence says of him:

> Math was able to hear without difficulty "every sound of speech that reached the air," he was utterly righteous and just in his dealings with gods and men, and was the great diviner, teacher and master of omens.

He has been equated with Manawyddan and Pryderi, and has none of the connotations associated with other pantheons' Gods of the Underworld, meaning he is rather beautiful, albeit dark and deep, and his methods of training are to enlighten rather than to judge.

Absolutely all of the Déithe are Threshold Dwellers, and Math is no exception.

The end of one cycle and the beginning of another is where he resides. Witches do not consider life and death as being absolutes, but are recognized as any specific change that has that appearance (for example, initiation in all its forms).

Math appears, bidden or unbidden, at times of transition—to assist in the rebirth, so to speak. He is cloaked in a mantle of crow or raven feathers, from head to foot; his hair and eyes are as dark as the bird he represents. He is also a shapeshifter and as such he may not appear as entirely human, but birdlike, or he may even appear as the bird itself. Despite being Déithe of the Underworld, he is especially invoked at, or just prior to, dawn. You will hear his voice in the first birdsong of the day, and the interpreting of omens is by way of what the birds say and/or the direction and "shape" of their flight.

At times he can be seen lying down with his feet in the lap of a maiden.

Some of his other names are Arawn, Blathnat, and definitely Don, and he is another persona of both Merlin and Taliesin.

Govannon

He is Déithe of the forge and shapeshifting.

All draíocht is a process of creativity and transformation. Smith-crafting is the quintessential transformative process. The smith begins with a lump of ore (the element of earth) and, utilizing the elements of Air, Fire, and Water, turns it into something else: the Song of the sword, cup, shield, spear, axe, talisman of gold, silver, bronze, pewter, platinum— dreaming forever of its own transformation.

This also is the process of alchemy required of witches: they must "smith" themselves by drawing out their potential and hammering out "impurities" to become what they innately know they are destined to become.

When you enter Mythos and meet with Govannon he will always appear as powerfully muscular, dirty, sweaty, charismatic. He is naked to the waist with only a leather apron covering (protecting) his genitals, and his body glows with the light of the forge. He has strong hands that are capable of the delicacy of a brain surgeon, for when he works with precious metals and gemstones he is capable of creating the finest detail.

He represents your imagination and your prowess, your capacity to consider the finest detail and the most difficult of decisions, and your ability to follow through with strength and determination on whatever task you have set.

The other name he is known by (in the Celtic pantheon) is Goibhniu.

Puck

> Jack do you never sleep, does the green still run deep in your heart? Or will these changing times, motorways, powerlines, keep us apart? Well, I don't think so—I saw some grass growing through the pavement today . . .
>
> —Jethro Tull, from "Jack in the Green"

Also known as Robin Goodfellow and Jack in the Green, no Imramma would be complete without the Trickster, the divine Fool, the Adversary, the Cunningman himself.

You can lead your whole life anticipating that it will serve you, be predictable, fulfill your ambitions, and you would be blind to the wildest of all wild things—the unexpected.

Puck is like the Coyote, like Loki of other pantheons, but he is utterly ours also. He can create mischief, disorder, and is the Lord of Misrule. As such, you can be sure that he'll turn up in your life sometime—summoned or otherwise.

I'm not going to give a description (he'd despise me for doing so!). I suggest you use your imagination, bearing in mind that he'll change to suit himself because he, also, is a shapeshifter, so he can appear as man, woman, child, animal, or unusual weather. He's where the other sock goes every time you do the washing and where the object sought went when you find it after having already looked there!

If you do not have a sense of humor or an acceptance of the fatedness of many things, then knowing Puck will assist you to develop such necessary gifts.

Herne (the Hunter)

Herne is the Great Lord of the Forest, the Avenger, not only the Hunter but also the Hunt itself.

He is the traditional Greenman (even Robin Hood), and his image has been carved by dedicated masons onto many of the cathedrals of Britain and Europe to keep his memory alive and to remind those oppressed by conquering regimes that eventually the draíocht and the Déithe will revoke the problem of their seeming annihilation. The Hounds of Herne are likened to the Fianna (and they're still here!).

He is barely seen when sought through draíocht, as he tends to blend with the Wild Woods, so seek the glint of his eye among the oak and ash, rowan and thorn, eucalypt, redwood, and saguaro.

Herne is invoked (*very* carefully) when accountability for extreme wrongs against the earth, and threats against any more overt destruction of the Green, is required.

Question: Where lie your allegiances?

I mention Herne the Hunter with a cringe of caution, ah! But then I relax—for have you yet discovered the draíocht to invoke the Wild Hunt? I will not be giving it to you; if that is what you seek here you are mistaken. The Hunt always catches the Hunted (or someone). The Hunt will not stop until a quarry is brought down.

He gets mixed up with Arthur, who, so sayeth certain legends, killed all the first-born in a seeming mistake.

Invoking Deíthe

Theory

To invoke one or other of the Déithe is to call upon them as an external agent and not as an archetype. To invoke is to seek contact, communication, and integration.

Until the time that a substantial contact has been made, you may be laboring without satisfaction—you can only ever learn so much from books and the opinions of others, and the reality is that draíocht will happen through personal experience and communication with the Worlds of Mythos.

The Déithe is to be invoked through the knowledge of (a) what it is that you want to know and learn, and (b) your advanced knowledge of what it is that you summon. The persona that you invoke must align, in concept and intent, with what you know; you must be prepared, by reiving, through focus and from within a ritual Circle, to ensure that you do not pick up stray energies, as these types of workings are like iron filings to a magnet.

To honor the Déithe that you invoke you are to keep adequate records of the encounter, seek knowledge and integration and not self-gain, and be prepared to follow through on the things that you learn. Do not just call them for the sake of curiosity or experimentation.

Therefore, you'll summon the persona of the Déithe, for the properties they represent, as follows:

Lugh: For the attunement and refinement of your own sense of personal power; in matters relevant to justice, decision-making, aspiration; to be adept at several things.

Artu: In matters relevant to hope, mediation, equilibrium, education, government, religion, inspiring others, and in excelling at strategy.

Hu: To assist you in the process of growth for any project that takes time for completion; to help you to "lighten up"; to develop a sense of humor; in understanding the seasons of the earth and what grows well with what.

Lancelet: In matters relevant to love; questing; justice pertaining to environmental damage; in battle (whatever the battle may be); in developing whatever martial art with which you train your body.

Merlin: He will advise you on what's relevant and what's not regarding so-called arcane knowledge; in seeing into the future; in recognizing what is the truth and what is the lie in any situation; in interpreting dreams and omens; in the art of glamouring.

Cernunnos: To advise you in all matters of power, of freedom, of sexuality. He is summoned in times of unjustified "attack"; to aid you in recognizing your totem and how to work with it; in matters of therianthropy (shapeshifting).

Gwydion: To aid you with the "sight"; analysis of emotional interference caused by conditioning; again, for the inspirations of the faidh; for illumination on any subject; in removing obstacles that stand in the way of research and knowing where to look for pertinent information.

Manannan: To see beneath the surface of things; to recognize deceit and illusion in any situation (including in yourself); to prophetically tap into the Anima; in all matters where you need protection or a cloak of invisibility; to protect those who travel/live by the sea.

Diancecht: In matters pertaining to health and well-being—of the self, others, and/or the environment; and in the development of patience.

Taliesin: To acquire the skills of the spoken or the written word; for any moves that are to take place; to assist the memory, in learning and oratory.

Math: He can be considered the male counterpart of the High Priestess card in the tarot; you will learn just about anything at his hands that he wishes to teach you, but "through a glass but darkly." As an Underworld Déithe he will choose the teaching that he wishes to impart without your conscious awareness. He can seem like an adversary. He'll dream you; you'll wake up wondering, What was that supposed to mean?

Bel: In matters relevant to individuality (in difference to the herd-mind) and practical, personal achievement. In matters relevant to honor; to come to really know yourself; to realize practical, personal achievement.

Govannon: When you need to develop sheer physical strength; in the acquisition of required objects; to transform one thing into another (literally); in understanding the properties of the elements.

Puck: To unsettle a situation; to cause a sometimes-needed bit of chaos; to challenge a pompous, dogmatic, know-it-all control-freak.

Herne: To seek (maybe once in your life—maybe never) vengeance against an obvious villain (like the politics that denies people the right to live peacefully in their tribal land; or that wants to fell old growth forests; or those against people who advocate vivisection; or regimes who harbor torturers; or those who think it's okay to use children for prostitution—shall I go on?).

11 Connection and Communication

He's watching me watching you watching him watching me
I'm watching you watching him watching me.

—Jethro Tull, "Watching Me Watching You"

Practice

Bathe with intent of purification.

Set up your Circle with the desired ritual tools upon the altar. You may want to include: candles (one for your altar and the other four for the elemental points at the outer edge of your Circle), chalice (water), wand (fire), athame (air), pentacle (earth), wine, special garment (if you wear one).

Read over the attributes of each persona of Déithe. When you have chosen the one that you want to come to know, you cast your Circle, invoke the elemental guardians, go into meditation to focus yourself (four-fold breathing or a soft, humming chant), consecrate the wine with chalice and athame, raise the chalice in honor of the Déithe, and drink of it.

Sit or kneel in such a manner as to be comfortable for a span of time, and prepare your mind for the visualization and invocation of the Déithe that you have chosen to work with.

When you are ready you will close your eyes and breathe deeply while seeing yourself in a setting that is conducive to the Déithe you seek contact with. Call him from that place and go with whatever you are there to experience until the ritual's conclusion.

When you return from the Otherworld and the contact you have experienced there, record what has occurred in your book.

Then farewell the guardians and banish the Circle.

Work at getting to know the many persona of Déithe over several months, even years. But *do* take your time, as too much enthusiasm can cause disruption in your life.

Part 5

The Wheel of the Solar/Earth Year (2)

12

The Rituals of
Solstice and Equinox

The Stag within you—wild! enchanted!
Lost on concrete streets that know no giving.

—Ly de Angeles, *The Feast of Flesh and Spirit*

Introduction

Dreams are sometimes the way we journey from one "place" and one "time" into another (I wrote a whole section on dreams in *Witchcraft: Theory and Practice,* so I won't repeat it here).

I remember dreaming that I took an old, fat woman, who was wearing a mauve chenille dressing gown, from the nursing home, where she'd been staying, to the train station. I asked the ticket man for two tickets to a place called Hampton. He informed me that there was only one left, but that one of us could pay at the other end. I bought that one ticket. We boarded the train and traveled until the train stopped at a halfway station where everyone could use the bathroom. I took the old woman into the bathroom . . . then I woke up.

That same morning my mother and I were drinking coffee out on the veranda, swapping dreams (as we did), when the phone rang. My mother took the call. It was her ex-husband's son informing her that his aunt, who we had only ever met twice, had died during the night in the nursing home where she had been for many years, and that we were invited to the funeral in two days. The service was to be held at a funeral home in the suburb of Hampton, Melbourne.

That was my first train dream. Many such dreams informed me of deaths over the years.

I had bus dreams, too. I used to dread those dreams, as they would always herald the circumstances leading to a change of residence. I haven't had them for years now, but I haven't moved house for years either.

The symbols that certain dreams express are the same symbols that we use in our waking "dreams"—our controlled visualizations. I have used the bus throughout the following journeys, and I mention it here because the symbolism is uncommon . . .

. . . but then, I'm not a textbook witch, so even the journeys will not fill the expectations of many who may be used to legends fitting some more ethereal prerequisite.

The bus indicates the (seeming) neverending changeability of the experience of the cycles of the earth. The bus is an incongruous symbol to use as a mystical vessel for journeying between the worlds, but it is perfectly acceptable, because the Déithe often have a sense, not only of humor, but also of the absurd, which is always so delightful because it's so easy to take serious things too seriously.

The legends that you are about to read are set in the day to day, for it needs to be understood that legends aren't about the past, they're about the sacred, which is living and ever-present.

None of the legends have a beginning or an ending, because what does? Every seeming beginning is the result of all that precedes it, and every ending is simply a pause between experiences.

The solstices and equinoxes can seem like fixed points in a solar year, whereas, in truth, they are realizations of an immortal procession.

The Déithe express themselves, throughout the legends, with human faces, because that's what they have asked of me here: they are as immortal as time. Their seeming normality and their seeming humanity are their gifts to you as you travel with them, so that you might understand that you could pass them on the street, and be touched in the passing, only to know it by the changes in your own life that occur as a result. You may never realize what happened, but that doesn't alter the fact that something wonderful is moving in the world, despite the bleak reporting on the world news.

Journeying Worlds

The rituals at the turning times of the solar/earth wheel are the solstices and equinoxes. Acknowledging them is to align you with these cycles, both personally and environmentally. The mythological symbolism is most important, as it allows you to personalize with the cycle and see the cycle as other than "out there." Being a witch is irrevocably bound up and interwoven with these progressions, as well as the fire festivals of Llugnassad, Samhain, the Feast of Bride (Imbolc), and Beltane.

It is also important to understand that earth, supporting as she does the myriad of diverse life forms, is Déithe. She is not just a piece of dirt to be exploited for her wealth, most of which, when left alone, creates a profound balance that we, at this stage of our conscious development, can only partially comprehend.

Midwinter Solstice: Meán Geimhridh [myawn gev-ri]
Also known as Yule; Alban Arthan.
    December 22; June 22 in the southern lands.

Spring Equinox: Meán Earraigh [myawn ah-ri]
Also known as Ostara; Alban Eiler.
    March 21; September 21 in the southern lands.

Midsummer Solstice: Meán Samhraidh [myawn sow-ri or sav-ri]
Also known as Litha; Alban Heruine.
    June 22; December 22 in the southern lands.

Autumn Equinox: Meán Fómhair [myawn fohw-er]
Also known as Mabon; Alban Elfed.
    September 21; March 21 in the southern lands.

These Sabbats are a recognition of a continuous *cyclic* nature of time. Contemplation of the continuum (Imramma) is necessary; they are not really four separate or isolated rituals, but markers that acknowledge an entire and continuous revolution.

At all times it is necessary to realize that the "seasons" are internal and otherworldly (the realm of Annwn), as well as environmental (the realm of Abred), as well as pan-dimensional (the realm of Gwynvyd), as well as eternal and immanent (the realm of Ceugant).

The Legends: Points of Theory

- Samhain initiates the onset of winter—the Winter Solstice is actually midwinter.

- Beltane initiates the onset of summer—the Summer Solstice is actually midsummer.

- The "'twixt and 'tween" is always the time of day and the times in a year when the veils between the worlds are at their finest, therefore allowing easier access in the crossing from one reality to another. In a day those times are between the day and the dark (dusk) and between the dark and the day (pre-dawn). In a year they are the solstices, the equinoxes, and the Fire Festivals, none more so than Samhain.

- The Midwinter Solstice represents the rebirth of the Sun King, the return of the Oak King, and the power of the Great Goddess to create and regenerate. It is a time for great rejoicing—it lets us know that nothing truly dies, that death is merely another function of life.

- The Midsummer Solstice represents the symbolic death of the Sun King, the battle between the Oak King and the Holly King, and the Holly King's time to reign. The Great Goddess is also the Reaper, and there's not one among us who is unaware that, despite the abundance of the season, the height of summer is the herald of the cold and the dark yet to come. It reminds us of our mortality—that everything dies and that it's okay, because it's in the nature of life.

- On the matter of the Quicken Brew and the bestowing of immortality on those who don't die during the process . . . this is symbolic of the rite of initiation. Once a witch, always a witch! The mention of those dying during the process refers to the few people who seek (and sometimes attain) initiation, either as a solitary or into a coven, who simply would like to be witches (for whatever reason) but are not. They don't literally experience body-death—all it means is that there is no quickening.

- On the matter of immortality—everything is immortal, it's just that some people are blind to this and, therefore, are afraid. No beginning, no end. The wheel spins and spins.

- Witchcraft is mundane (from the Latin root *mundus*: meaning "world"), no matter what is studied. What this means is that we have no concept of "a better place" or getting "off the wheel" (an Eastern concept associated with attaining dharma). I have heard so many people put the world down as being "not as good" as whatever equivalent of heaven they aspire to, and because of this they are ambivalent toward life. Witches simply maintain that there is more than one world to explore. The legends of the solstices and the equinoxes are set in the mundane worlds. Several of them. Everyone within the legends is real.

The Ritual of the Midwinter Solstice: Meán Geimhridh
Requirements for the Ritual

Gather the usual things, plus a consecrated oil of storax, amber, and oak-moss; incense of sandalwood; oil of nightqueen; seasonal festive food; a fireplace or brazier. Gather deadwood to burn during the ritual.

Set up for the ritual in the usual manner, and bathe with intent of purification.

When you are ready you will seat yourself before the altar, light the altar candle and the incense, and center yourself by using four-fold breathing, leading to a soft, humming chant.

Use your Staff to cast a Circle about yourself, saying:

> *O Circle of draíocht, outside of time,*
> *keep all within and all without*
> *and forge a barrier between them.*
> *I seek to journey beyond the Veil.*
> *Be ye cast in the names of N . . . (the Lady and Lord),*
> *By Earth, by Sky, by Sea!*

Using your wand and athame, invoke the guardians of the Four Gates.

Go to the altar and refuel the incense. Be still. Use whatever technique you have been practicing to prepare for the journey.

Read the Legend of the Winter Solstice, personalizing with all the characters in the story, for the entirety.

When you have done so and can feel the Déithe within yourself, you'll continue the ritual to its conclusion.

Please note: these legends are probably not what you'd expect. They are the result of the desire on the part of the Déithe to express a decidedly contemporary ancientness. I was incredibly surprised when I wrote them. They are, after all, not about doing draíocht, but *being* it, and are therefore written in a common tongue.

> *The journey into Mythos is as follows:*

The Solstice of Midwinter

> Jack do you never sleep?
> Does the Green still run deep in your heart?
>
> —Jethro Tull, from "Jack in the Green"

The power's been going on and off all day. It's a good thing the boss decided the 'open-fire' look would please the customers. Pub's been packed all night, everybody trying to keep warm.

"Lot of people gonna freeze in this weather," says Fergus as he locks the doors on the last of the patrons before the patrol cars cruise their rounds and fine him (again!) for being open after hours.

"You go on home, Rowan." He comes back and starts shifting the last of the glasses into the dishwasher, "and be careful out there—the cold's bloody tragic."

No one has ever known the temperature to get this low, and everybody in the pub had talked about little else. "Weird . . ." someone said. "Unnatural, I reckon," said another. "It's those bleedin' scientists have gone and played around with it, I figure!" had been the reply.

Yep. People going to die on a night like this.

I throw on my extra sweater and load myself with coat and beanie and gloves and scarf.

"G'night boss," I call over my shoulder as I pull open the door onto the street, slamming it locked behind me.

It's like walking into a furnace only the other way 'round. The wind tears at my coat, sleet bites into my eyes. I have to stop and pull my scarf up over my mouth and nose so that I can even breathe. I start the seven-block walk to home, cursing wherever the cabs have all gone.

I have to work hard just to put one foot in front of the other. I can't feel my feet and I'm only managing to keep my hands even slightly warm by shoving them into my armpits. Even the scarf around my face feels frozen after a minute.

Gonna move somewhere else, I say to myself—but then I've been saying that for years and have never been able to come up with enough money or enough courage to do it. No work anywhere else anyway—not in this city, not in any, anymore.

Three a.m.'s a bitch, I think.

I ignore the Don't Walk signs at the street crossings—no one else's stupid enough to be out on a night like this. Street's deader than the grave, even with Christmas just four days away.

I've just crossed over Market Street and I'm about to turn onto Left Bank Road that leads onto the turnoff to the last five blocks to my place (two rooms above the Chinese Cafe down by the canal), when this big guy moves out of the alley and blocks my way.

I'm freaked. I look up into coal-black eyes, pinning me to the spot.

He's easy six-two, six-three, bundled in a big old army greatcoat. I can't figure out if he has layers and layers of clothes underneath or whether he's just plain huge. Dark skin, little plaited beard, no hat, ragged dreds studded all through with black feathers hanging halfway to his waist.

I don't know if he's going to kill me, rob me, or try to bum a cigarette, but whatever blood's left unfrozen in my veins kinda just freezes altogether and I don't know whether I could run even if my legs weren't shaking, or whether my bladder's just going to end up embarrassing me.

"Wh . . . ?" I stammer, "Ah, 'scuse me."

My attempt at being casual—at walking around him—is blocked as he moves his bulk and puts a hand on my arm to prevent any attempt to avoid him.

"Name's Hunter," he says softly, deeply. "Need your help. Got a job for you."

His eyes are like the eyes of a raptor. I'm not about to get out of this, I think flatly. The wind's ripping and jagging all around him, but the big man's body is blocking it from tearing at me.

"What?" I say, resigned. He takes hold of the sleeve of my coat and walks me into the alley. I never go this way; have no idea where it leads. There's garbage and refuse, pallets and dead cars, dumpsters and stacks of boxes—refugees from the back of unknown shops.

We're walking for several minutes. Wow, I think, this place is a bloody maze! It's a warren of twisting turns—back alleys leading into other back alleys—no idea where I am. Hoping this guy knows where he's going 'cause I sure don't. Wondering whether he's just dragging out the inevitability of some weirdo perversity.

Five, ten minutes, it takes us. Black as pitch.

Hunter seems sure of where he's going. Walls like prisons all around. Frozen to the marrow by now.

He jerks me to a stop and slides open a big heavy door. He flicks a switch and the boxy little entrance is lit up dimly by a naked bulb hanging from a wire suspended from the low ceiling. He wrenches the rusty industrial door closed and flips the bar locked.

"What's your name boy?" he asks, as he reaches under his coat and pulls out a small red plastic flashlight.

"Ah, it's Rowan—I'm Rowan. Wh-what's going on?" I feel like a rabbit stuck in the lights of an oncoming truck. And I still can't feel my feet.

"Thought it'd be you," says Hunter. He hasn't smiled yet. "How serious is this?" I ask.

"You know," he replies.

I'm really frustrated; starting not to feel so afraid anymore.

"What are you talking about!" I yell. Is this guy some crazy?

"Don't raise your voice." He grabs my face in his enormous hands and squeezes my cheeks. "Just . . ." Oh, oh, I think.

"Look," he sighs, "just don't raise your voice okay?" and he lets go.

"Sorry . . ." he says softly, "let's just keep going okay?"

We start down the stairs. Soon the light from the top landing gets lost in the darkness and Hunter flicks on the torch. There's a sense of urgency that comes at me from him. He's hurrying.

In the constantly moving swathe of the torch's light the place looks like the kind of place that used to lead to trains or something. Same smell but unused—mold or damp or something else living in the dark. Old tiles on the walls in places, or else that disgusting gray-green paint that nobody uses anymore. The stairs are just concrete. I feel like I'm going to die here. A manmade tomb a long way down.

Hunter's not talking and I'd rather not think—it's too late and I'm too unnerved. I start counting steps between the landings—twenty-eight, landing's thirty; twenty-nine, landing's thirty. Fifth lot down and we're at the bottom.

The beam from the flashlight makes the dark feel like some kind of monster.

"Shit, I'd never make a miner," I say, just to break the unbelievably dense silence. He chuckles. Alright! I think, breakthrough!

We're on the platform of some abandoned part of the Underground. We drop down onto the tracks and Hunter leads us into one of the tunnels.

"Watch your step," he says, shining the beam onto the ground. The tracks are littered with chunks of rubble. He throws the light up onto the wall and I can see how the whole lot looks like it could cave in any minute—great slabs have already fallen off. Yeah, I'll be quiet.

We walk maybe a hundred yards down the tunnel before I notice the warm, yellow light just up ahead to the left.

We get to the entrance of what looks like a service bay and Hunter jumps up onto the ledge, pulling me up behind him. It's a cavernous concrete room lit by dozens of candles and a few kerosene storm lanterns.

My mouth drops open as I look around (aware of a momentary whimper from somewhere).

First few seconds:

The original fixtures of the service bay are still here—a thick cloth hose with a dull brass nozzle, wound up and hanging from one wall beside several hooks; bench underneath it. Shelves line the back wall with old paint tins, jars, and rusted stuff that I don't recognize; an antique metal and laminated table stands in the corner with cups and plates, a half-empty jar of instant coffee, sugar and a carton of milk; a three-ring cooker attached to a gas bottle is on the floor beneath the table, along with other things. A tap and a sink and what looks like an old kerosene fridge are against the other wall.

Someone's scrounged up furniture. There's an overstuffed three-seater settee covered in dark brown velvet—pretty thread-bare mostly—in the middle of the room, right beside a cut down forty-four gallon drum with holes knocked into it, glowing red and sending out a welcome haze of warmth. Beside it is a tub overflowing with bits of wood and scavenged timber.

In front of the settee someone's organized a couple of crates and planks that make up a squat table, and there's an assortment of straight-backed chairs and a couple of arm-chairs on this side of the table.

Over by the other wall are several mattresses—bedding and pillows in disarray—attesting to the fact that there's probably more than just Hunter staying down here.

He strips off his coat and gloves and piles them just inside the entrance. I follow his lead.

"Okay," I start, "Can you please tell me . . ." He ignores me as a small moan, followed by rapid breathing, breaks the silence of the room and Hunter strides quickly over toward the settee, me right behind him.

On the floor, pushed up against the back of the couch, is a mattress, pillows piled up and covers disregarded. Two women are there, one sitting on the side of the mattress and the other propped up against the pillows, very pregnant and oh, wow! She's the most beautiful woman I have ever seen. She's got light red hair, all long and curly and messy, and ivory skin covered all over with a mist of freckles. She looks up at Hunter and smiles a smile at him that I'd die to have smiled at me. Hunter sits down beside her, dark skin beside pale, and takes her hand in his and lifts it to his lips like a prince would with his lady.

Then she looks at me. I'm melting! Her eyes have almost no color in the dim light—just a pale pale hazel that is hardly there at all. I stand there feeling conspicuous.

"I found him, Puck," he says to her softly. Then he addresses the older woman, still sitting side-on to me, long fingers stroking stray hairs from the younger woman's slightly sweaty face.

"How far apart?" he asks.

"Still twenty minutes, give or take," she replies with a deep, earthy voice. "Long time yet. Maybe the morning," and she gets up and stretches and walks over to me while Hunter snuggles close into Puck's body.

"Let's have a dram," as she takes my hand and draws me, staring, round to the settee. She reaches into one of the crates supporting the low table and brings up a good-labeled quart of *uiske beatha* and two shot glasses. While she's pouring I continue to stare. Black hair woven into hundreds of braids, tattoos all over her face and hands, earrings hanging from both ears, each different from the other but both looking like they're maybe made of bronze, both with little dark-red and dark-green gemstones winking in the light of the candles. She's wearing a black jumper two sizes too big for her tiny body and a pair of loose ex-army khakis tucked into calf high lace-ups. She's also kinda beautiful, but in a really strange way.

She hands me one of the shot glasses. "Slànte!" she grins, touching her glass to mine, "I'm Brighid."

She downs the strong drink in one mouthful and pours another. "So I guess you're wondering about all this."

"God, yes," I reply, just sipping.

"Well, you're the Rowan, aren't you." Not a question. "So you're gonna help us . . ."

Another moan and the sounds of Hunter guiding Puck's short puffing breaths.

"Time?" calls Brighid.

"Same," replies Hunter, holding up a little clock so that Brighid can check.

She turns back to me. I must look a mess. My nose is running as it thaws out and I try not to be too obvious as I wipe my sleeve over my face. I'm tired to death and feel like an abused dishrag on a comedown as the adrenaline settles from crazy to calm.

Brighid pulls out a wad of tissues from the pocket of her trousers and hands me some.

"I'm sure I'll be crying before this thing's over," she says, "but you deserve some. They're clean," she assures me as I hesitate. I grin sheepishly and turn my head to blow.

"See, the Rowan's got to bear witness." Full stop. Just that.

"I'm *so* lost," I say emphatically. "I've got *no* idea what I'm doing here, Brighid!"

Right when I'm about to hear the point of this whole weird thing there's the sound of voices, and boots crunching on gravel, coming from the tracks.

I look at Brighid, but she just pats my hands and says, "It'll wait, don't lose the plot . . ." and she rises to greet the newcomers. I sigh.

Four more people jump up onto the ledge and come into the room, chattering and laughing, and head straight for the fire, dumping an assortment of instruments onto the chairs around them and stripping off coats and hoods and scarves. Three men, one woman.

"Whoosh!" says one guy to Brighid as she pours more shots for the others, "wee chilly out, ma'am." Brighid chuckles as the others chatter over each other in excitement.

"It's begun," she says quietly.

Silence. Another moan from behind the settee. "Same!" calls Hunter. Nothing from the others—they just look at Brighid with what looks like wonder in their eyes.

"How was the gig?" asks Brighid, knowing that it really didn't matter to them anymore.

"When?" asks one of the men.

" 'Bout two hours ago," she replies. She looks at me and grins, "but we found the Rowan!"

They all move round and start shaking my hands and slapping me on the back. The girl with them, short, ragged, with spiky plum-colored hair, big brown eyes, and too much makeup, pushes them aside and holds out her hand for me to shake.

"Rude, aren't they?" she says as she grips my hand like she wants to arm-wrestle. "I'm called Black Annis." She tilts her head to the others, "and this here's Willie and Trev and Matt. We're the band!"

"Oh, yeah, I guessed that," I say lamely.

"And I'm the harper," she says proudly, "and we just played a gig without Puck and we *still* pulled it off!" She raises her voice just enough so that Puck could hear. "*Still pulled it off!*" she chortles.

"Don't raise your voice!" calls Hunter.

Black Annis puts one arm through mine and the other through Brighid's and leads us to the sofa where she plops us all down in a heap.

The other guys are hanging some of their instruments on the hooks beside the hose and laying others on the bench. I catch sight of a bodhrán and Black Anis' harp but miss seeing the rest.

"So we're the band," continues Black Annis, "and we call ourselves Fianna—and this here's our manager," she says, looking at Brighid, who laughs, "and I gather you've been introduced to Puck and Hunter."

"Duh," I answer.

"Hah!" she laughs, eager that I seem not to be too upset. "Hunter's our bodyguard, and all 'round leader you might say."

"*You* might say!" says Brighid, feigning indignation.

"What in God's name is going on here?" I plead, despairing of getting a clear answer from anyone.

"Don't take my name in vain," I hear from the big man behind the settee, followed by the sounds of Puck in the grip of another contraction.

"Annis, tell him," says Matt sitting around the other side of the table.

"They're in love, you see?" says Annis. "Love," and she snuggles up closer to me.

"It's been a long time," says Willie, joining us and downing a glass of the uiske beatha.

"Long time," echoes Matt.

"What?" I feel like the word's become my mantra and I'm stuck with it.

Brighid turns my face to hers. "No one might know about tonight. No one 'cept you, Rowan. And that'd be wrong!" I wait. Annis snuggles deeper. I like her—she's growing on me.

"See Puck's a human woman, even though she'll never go back—not now, 'cause of Hunter, you see? 'Cause of the child. And 'cause she doesn't want to anyway."

I'm gone. I'm lost. So I just wait.

Puck and Hunter get up from behind the settee. "I need to move a bit," says Puck.

Brighid gets up to go to her. "'S okay, I'm fine," Puck reassures the older woman.

She gives Hunter a little push away, "Go sit," she says to the big man, him pushing the dreds away from his face. "Make a coffee or something useful—keep yourself awake," she smiles. I can see he doesn't want to be away from her and I wonder at how much he'd borne to come out into the night and find me. And I was still none the wiser as to why. Hunter watches from the arm of the settee as Puck caresses her own belly.

"Hey, hey!" says Annis, turning my face back from the vision that's Puck. "She's taken!"

"I know that," I say defensively, looking at Hunter who's looking down at me.

Then he smiles for the first time and it's the biggest, whitest, healthiest set of teeth I've ever seen, only made a little unnerving by the length of the canines.

"I can understand him, Annis," he says, "leave the poor boy be."

"Look me. Look me, Rowan!" says Annis, bouncing.

"Okay," I say, grinning at her. "You're pretty cute for a girl." She chortles with pleasure. I wonder at how comfortable I'm feeling with these crazies.

I turn back to Brighid. "Like you were saying?"

"Puck's human."

I must be looking stupid or something. "And . . . ?" I say, thinking this is all one big joke somehow.

"And we're not," she replies seriously.

"And you're . . . ?"

"We're the People," she replies, as though I ought to understand.

When it's obvious I don't, she says, "The People. The land, you know?" I'm shaking my head, little quick shakes.

Her mouth forms a thin, determined line.

"We're the People! The land. The forests. Wolves and things; ravens and seals and all. All of it—understand me, Rowan." She's frowning.

"What," I smile. "Like the Little People?"

"Do we look little to you?" says Hunter calmly.

"N-no."

"But we get called that," says Trev in my defense.

"You're on the right track," Willie backs him up.

"You telling me you're like the fair folk out of the legends?" I blurt, getting ready to laugh at the joke.

Puck contracts again, much sooner than the last time. Hunter goes to help her through it.

No one's laughing at the joke. They're all just looking at me.

"This is not fair . . . !" I start to say.

Brighid interrupts the beginning of my tirade, "This is the first time . . ." she takes a breath, ". . . this is the *first* time in over a thousand years that a mortal woman's taken one of our kind to love."

The others smile, great beaming smiles, and Annis puts her arms around me and nuzzles my neck.

"And it's the first time since I can remember—and I'm really old, Rowan" (I look at her—forty maybe?) "—that a baby's to come of it, and a boy for sure 'cause I can tell from the way it lies; and it's the first time since the Quicken got cut down that a baby boy gets born from one of you and one of us at the Winter's Solstice!" Tears well up, unshed. She wipes them away furiously.

"And you're the Rowan—and you're the witness," says Annis softly into my ear.

"So there's hope," says Hunter from over near the fire where he holds his Puck so gently.

"So there's hope . . ." echoes Brighid.

The journey ends.

Take time to come back before continuing the ritual.

Take up the consecrated wine, sprinkle a little on the food, and drink from the chalice. If there is another or others with you, you will share the food and wine with them.

Light the wood in the brazier or fireplace from the altar-flame, saying:

I light a beacon to light the Worlds
The Seasons change—the Roots of Life
I honor my ancient inheritance—
The freedom to Dance the draíocht
With all who Dance to the Piper!

To complete the Rite, you will raise the staff aloft and say:

The Sacred Seed beneath the Snow
I call Blessed the Darkness as I call Blessed the Light!
I call on the Déithe to reclaim the Lands

In the name of N . . . (the Déithe to whom you are allied),
By Mórrigan and all her Daughters—
By Earth, by Sky, by Sea
By the Sacred Law of Three!

Complete the ritual by farewelling the guardians and undoing the Circle as on previous occasions. Put away all ritual things and record any relevant information in your grimoire, then party.

The Ritual of the Spring Equinox: Meán Earraigh
Requirements for the Ritual

You will need the usual things, plus a consecrated oil of storax, amber, and oakmoss; incense of sandalwood; oil of nightqueen; seasonal festive food; a fireplace or brazier. Gather deadwood to burn during the ritual.

Set up for the ritual in the usual manner, and bathe with intent of purification.

When you are ready you will seat yourself before the altar, light the altar candle and the incense, and center yourself by using four-fold breathing leading to a soft, humming chant.

Use your staff to cast a Circle about yourself, saying:

O Circle of draíocht, outside of time, keep all within and all without
and forge a barrier between them.
I seek to journey beyond the Veil.
Be ye cast in the names of N . . . (the Lady and Lord),
By Earth, by Sky, by Sea!

Using your wand and athame, invoke the guardians of the Four Gates.

Go to the altar and refuel the incense. Be still. Use whatever technique you have been practicing to prepare for the journey.

Read the Legend of the Spring Equinox, personalizing with all the characters in the story for the entirety.

When you have done so, and can feel the Déithe within yourself, you'll continue the ritual to its conclusion.

The journey into Mythos is as follows:

Spring Equinox

> Pass the Cup and pass the Lady
> Pass the plate to all who hunger
> Pass the wit of ancient wisdom
> Pass the cup of crimson wonder . . .

> —Jethro Tull, from "Cup of Wonder"

I let my hand rest gently, reverently, on the book of spells my mother has left me. I feel stupid—Who am I kidding? I think.

The room's a mess. I hadn't bothered to bank up the old slow combustion stove before I'd gone to bed last night, so it's as dead as the garden. I walk out onto the porch, sighing, and sit down on the steps with my two mongrels—Jessie and Mate, slow-wagging their tails beside me—and I look out over the dusty morning.

The sunrise is very red. Another bad day.

I wonder, just like everyone else I've talked to, just where the rains have gone. Supposed to come down weeks ago. Weeks.

Nip in the air and the ravens are calling up the day.

If I'm going to try to work the old magic I ought to believe in it—isn't that how it goes?

Cecilly did. Everybody trusted her—everybody 'round here, despite whatever they might have thought of us among themselves.

No rain. Too long. Winter's near over, and the weatherman can call it El Niño or whatever he likes—it makes us all wonder what summer's going to bring. No, I think, better not even contemplate.

No point planting the good seed because the way things stand it's all just going to blow away.

I pull the blanket tighter around me as the dawn wind raises goose flesh on my arms.

Pretty lonely.

Oh well, nothing for it, I think. Later on today I'll dance the spell. Works or it doesn't.

Just like that, I make up my mind.

"Buena," I say to the dogs.

It's too early to go to town—might as well get the damned stove started and have a cup of coffee.

I'm just getting up to go inside when I see the dust of a vehicle churning up the road leading to my place. Not expecting anyone, 'specially not at this hour. Me and the dogs wander over toward the gate. The hens hear our footsteps and come "bock-bocking" out from under the house, demanding breakfast. "Hiss 'em," I call to the dogs who oblige by running them off 'til I know what's going on.

Yep, coming this way, sure is. Looks like a big old bus.

I'm just leaning on the fence when this thing that looks like it shouldn't be allowed to be on the road pulls into the gate and stops.

Hmm. I figure I ought to be a little wary but I've gone and left the shotgun up at the house. The dogs don't seem alarmed—Mate isn't even bothered to stand up while Jessie's got that stupid look she gets when she figures someone's come just to see her.

The door opens. First off this young guy comes out, lookin' pretty ordinary in jeans and a duffel coat—clean-shaven, nice open-kinda face— but then this weirdo little woman, no more'n five foot one or two, all covered in tattoos, and with those long fancy braids in her hair like the African women sometimes have (only this woman's white), drops down after him and I look down at the dogs, hoping they'll growl a warning or something. Nothing.

The woman takes the lead and comes right on over, bold as brass, and squats down to ruffle the fur around Jessie's neck like Jessie's a little safe pet or something when she looks as much like a big old wolf as you'd ever want to see. Stupid dog's rolling on her back.

"Beautiful morning," she says to me, looking up.

"Whatever . . ." I answer coolly. "Can I help you?"

"We're on tour," pipes up the guy, walking over to me with his hand held out. "Name's Rowan." I shake his hand with what I hope's a challenging grip.

"What are you, a rock band or somethin'?" I ask, looking at the bus and figuring they couldn't be very successful at it.

"No—folk-kinda music," says the woman, standing up.

"Just you two?" I ask, eyeing the bus once again.

"The others are still sleeping," she replies. "There's nine of us."

Alarm bells. "You're a long way outta town," I say frankly, "you need directions or somethin'?"

"We've just come from there," says Rowan, "everything's still shut up. No motel."

"Small town," I reply.

"We were wondering if you could maybe put us up out here?" he asks.

I guess I must be looking like I'm dumb or struck deaf. "Sir?" he asks again.

I laugh. "You're kidding, right?" I say.

"We wouldn't get in your way or anything," says the woman, ". . . oh, sorry! My name's Brighid by the way."

She holds out this little hand all covered in intricate spirals and triscele tattoos for me to shake. What can I do? So I shake her hand and it's surprisingly firm—not forced either.

"We could help out a bit 'til we get paid for some gigs—then we could pay our way," she adds enthusiastically.

I gesture around me at the old house and barn and utilities sheds. All had seen seriously better days but probably long before I was born.

"'Do I look like I've got room for guests?" I try to keep a straight face.

"Something about the place," says Brighid. "I felt it from the road. It's a good place."

"Been better," I shrug. "You some kinda mystic, lady?" I ask sarcastically. Then she smiles at me. Oh my, I think.

"Some kind, yeah," she replies.

Whatever.

"Look," I say, "it's early. You can come on up to the house if you want and I can make us some coffee and I'll see if I can think."

That smile again.

We wander back over to the house, assaulted by the hens on the way. I excuse myself for just a minute and grab the feed box from the porch to keep the girls quiet. Rowan and Brighid just stand there waiting 'til I come back.

We walk on into my house and I'm really embarrassed at the mess but I figure that once I get the fire started and the percolator on I'll give it a quick going over. Doesn't really matter I suppose—it's not like I'm entertaining or anything—but Cecily would have been disgusted with me.

"'Scuse the state of the place," I say, moving books, more books, my writing things and my notebooks, off the couch and dumping them on the floor beside. "Sit if you feel like it."

Brighid comes over to me, "You get the coffee sorted and I'll light the stove, okay?"

"It's a bitch of a thing, lady." I answer.

"I'm good with a fire," she replies with a twinkle in her eyes. She squats down and starts stacking the kindling in a neat little criss-cross in the grate.

"Suit yourself," I say, impressed.

I pull three mugs down from the cupboard along with the canister in which I keep my good Italian coffee—my pleasure, you know?—and I measure out enough for that perfect first brew of the day. "You take milk and sugar?" I ask over my shoulder.

"Yeah, two sugars and milk," replies Rowan.

"No," says Brighid, "black's perfect."

"You read all this stuff?"

I turn back to Rowan who's stacking my books in a tidy pile, looking at the titles as he does so.

"Yeah," I reply defensively. Nobody 'round here's interested in my passion—history, mythology, the supernatural and the like. I stopped trying to talk about it with anybody years ago.

"Hmm," says Rowan, looking at one in particular—the one on Fionn McCumhail called *The Master of Earth and Water.*

"I've read this one," he says, smiling, "like it a lot."

Huh? I think, surprised.

"What's your name?" Brighid asks me.

"Jack Forester, ma'am," I tell her.

"Grr! How about 'Jack Forester, *Brighid*,'" she says, lifting an eyebrow, eyes twinkling. "How long you lived here, Jack?"

"All my life Brighid. Lived here with my mother 'til she died a few years ago."

"On your own?" she continues.

"Got the dogs," I reply, thinking, This is none of your business, lady.

"Just the two of you was there?"

Here I go. I'm not about to talk about this with them. Always people had things to say about Cecilly's never having been married and all; calling me a bastard when I went to school—that and other bad things—'til I stopped going and started learning from home when the chores were done. Not going to. Loved her so much. So I don't answer.

Fire's going strong. Good fire. I lift the iron plate off the stove and put the percolator on and straight away start shoving mess into the corners, out of the way, and straightening the covers on the other couch over under the window that I use for a bed. Couldn't be bothered with the bedrooms; for me it's easier just to live in one room.

Shit! I realize that I'd left the book of spells wide open in plain sight on the covers of my bed. I grab it up and kinda sidle out of the room and down the hallway leading to the bedrooms and the bathroom (for what it is) and open the closet door where I shove it way back on the top shelf.

When I come back into the living room Brighid's already poured the steaming coffee into the mugs. She hands me one, then Rowan, then squats down beside the stove, keeping warm.

"Yo!" I hear from the porch.

Rowan grins and gets up, stumbling over his own feet, calling, "In here!"

In walks this punky kinda girl with her hair all done up in parrot-colored dyes, sticking out every which way, dressed all in black, stomping through the doorway in boots that shoulda been on a man's feet. Rowan gets to her and puts his arms around her and she snuggles into him like they're used to the fit of each other.

This makes three, I think to myself. Another sigh.

"Grab some coffee if you want, love," I say to her as they come over near the fire. She does.

Rowan sits back down and picks up another book that he'd been flipping through before the parrot-girl came in. "Wouldn't mind borrowing this," he says. It's one of my books on local lore about ghosts and hauntings.

I'm not about to let any of my books go into the hands of some stranger so I don't answer.

"I can smell it on you!" says the parrot-girl cryptically. I blush and scowl and wonder if living out here alone for so long hasn't had its effect.

"Shh!" hisses Brighid, "don't be so quick, Annis!" as Rowan clamps a hand over her mouth. She giggles at him, squirming.

"I apologize if I'm offending you," I add in my own defense, "but it's not as though I'd invited any of you."

Jessie bellies over to me, momentarily leaving Brighid's lap, and I crouch down to stroke her tawny red coat, wishing they'd all just go away.

"Jack, this is Annis," says Brighid, "and she's got a mouth, as you'll find out the longer you know her, but she means no harm. She doesn't mean you smell."

"What then?"

"Little magics," says Annis. "There's little magics all over you Jack."

"Don't know what you're on girl," I imply, "but you better not be bringing any o' that stuff onto my property." I drain my cup. "So now, I've got a lot to do—so if you'd all . . ."

What's that? *Thunk, thunk, schruuuch* from outside.

"What the . . ." I get up and head for the door knowing, just knowing, that one or more of the others from the bus are mucking around my place.

I bolt over the porch and down the steps looking around for them. Can't see 'em. Then I hear it again: *thunk, thunk*. The others are behind me.

The noise is coming from my garden patch. I stride 'round the side of the house and there, in what ought to be my early spring vegetable and herb garden, is this huge black guy, stripped to the waist, dreds all tied up on top of his head, tattoos darker than his skin, all wavering like serpents over his big-muscled body. He's mattocking up the beds, while another guy—fair skin, long, flame-colored hair tied in two plaits, more tattoos— just goes along behind him with my rake, smoothing out what the big guy's turned over.

"What do you think you're *doing!*" I yell. Oh, look, there's more of 'em sitting on the ground inside the fence that keeps the beasts from my patch—two men, a very attractive young woman and a—a baby at her breast! Oh, mother! I think, Now what?

The big guy and the red-haired guy are already sweating despite the sun just up and the nip in the air.

"Turning your ground," says the big guy seriously.

"Smoko!" says the other pulling a pouch of makings out of the pocket of his jeans as he ambles over to the others.

I'm fuming! Who do they think they are? Would've had to have rummaged in my own barn for the mattock and the rake.

Crowded. They've got me crowded—bloody nerve!

Bunch of strung-out city weirdos, I'm thinking as I gauge the odds. Doesn't matter if they kill me, I'm not going down meek. This is *my* place.

"Get out! Get out the lot of you!" I yell, turning from the three behind me to the others over the fence.

The big guy shoulders the mattock and comes toward me, looking straight at me with the blackest eyes I've seen outside of an animal.

He opens the gate and comes over, lowers the mattock and leans on the handle (and I thought I was tall!). "Can't do that," he says straight.

"Wh-what?" I say stupidly, dead scared as he looms over me. Nope. Won't be put down.

"I want you all to get back on the bus and leave," I say emphatically.

"Can't," he replies quietly.

I'm dumbfounded. "Why not?"

"You're not ready," he replies.

"For *what!*" I say.

"For the rain," says Brighid, coming to stand beside me and looking up at me with those eyes. "You're not ready for the rain, Jack."

I look into those pale silver-gray eyes, wishing I'd known her when I was a younger man; wishing she didn't look quite so weird, anyway; wishing she'd come alone.

"I was . . ." I stop myself sharply. *What am I doing?* I was just about to blab about doing the spell!

"Look around you, woman," I say. "Does it bloody-well look like rain to you?"

"It'll rain," says the big guy, rubbing his hands on his army surplus pants and holding one out for me to shake. "I'm Hunter. The guy with the rake's Willie, the lady's name's Puck and our son's Robin. The lazy guys are Matt and Trevor."

I shake his hand unwillingly. Not a shred of threat reaches me from any of them.

"Jack," I say.

"Figures," he replies. He reaches up and undoes the cord that's keeping his dreds back and they fall down around him like live things—looks like he's got about two dozen black-bird feathers mixed in with them.

"You really ought to loosen up, Jack," he says. "Can I grab a drink of water or something—throat's pretty dry already."

This whole thing's got me mind-rackingly confused, so what's this little bubble of excitement—this little thread of real pleasure—that's kinda sneaking up on me? Things around here are desperate. I must be loco to be even considering having them stay awhile.

Later on that morning I pick up the keys off the hook inside the barn and *yee-up* the dogs onto the back of the truck.

Hunter's back in the patch working it hard, like it's his own, and his lady, what's her name?—oh yeah, Puck—well Puck, along with the other two guys, are up at the house working at fixing a stack of food. From their own supplies.

I've got to go into town and organize water deliveries to come and fill up my near-depleted tanks—doesn't matter if these people think rain's coming, I'm not risking it.

I crank over the engine when Rowan yells "Wait up!" from the porch. He comes running across the yard asking if I'm going into town. When I tell him yeah, he asks if some of them can get a ride in with me to see about supplies and to maybe set up a gig somewhere.

"Won't be long," he says, going off to get the others.

He comes back with Annis and Brighid and Matt and Willie. Brighid and Willie pull themselves up into the cab with me, and the others hop up onto the tray along with the dogs.

We're driving along causing a sky full of dust behind us and Willie pulls out this little tin whistle from his pocket and starts playing a reel. Brighid keeps looking at me and grinning. Must admit by the time we get into town I'm smiling to myself and tapping on the wheel like a kid.

I stop the truck outside of Blake's Farm Supplies to the jaw-dropping faces of two local women sitting on the seat out front. Brighid comes with me while the others go off to the pub to try to convince the proprietor into letting them play there.

Inside Tom Blake's telling Marty Swain that the water deliveries are backed up until after the weekend. I wait, resigned to the same story. Brighid's got her arm hooked through mine, and I'm feeling pretty good about that when Tom and Marty look up from the order book. They see me standing there with Brighid and I figure I know what they're thinking, but by now that warm bubble I felt in the truck's spread out through my whole self and I just don't care. They're not about to say anything to my face anyway—country folk always wait 'til you're not around.

"Morning Tom," I say casually. "Three days you say for the tankers?"

"Ah, yeah, Jack." He clears his throat. "You ordering?"

"Tsk, tsk," whispers Brighid quietly.

"What?" I say looking down at her.

"Nothing, Jack. Doesn't matter," she replies sighing.

"Put me down to get both my tanks filled up, will you Tom? Got company for a while."

Tom looks at me like I'm a fool, shrugs and pushes his glasses up his nose, and writes up the order. Marty's staring at Brighid, then smirking at me. Tom's mumbling under his breath.

"Anything else?" he asks dryly.

"Just the water . . . thanks Tom," I say, turning us toward the door.

"Monday, Jack," he relies.

"Whatever, Tom . . ." and I pull the door shut deliberately without slamming it.

My jaw's all clenching and unclenching. Brighid stops us and looks at me.

"Some place we can sit and drink something cold while we wait for the others?" She's tactful, I'll say that for her.

We walk over to the cafe, take a couple of chairs at a table, and I order us cold apple juices from the waitress. She's smiling at Brighid, who's smiling back.

When she's gone Brighid turns to me and takes both my hands in her own. "Been hard has it, Jack?" she asks.

"Don't wanna talk about it," I say.

"Annis is right Jack. There's little magics all around you . . . and the things you read? Humph. Seems to me you don't fit the picture you're trying so hard to fit." Eyes as soft as dawn on a pond, she's got. I just sort of start talking.

"Mother's name was Cecilly," I say. "Came here with me in her belly already, and started out renting that house I live in now. Don't know how she managed at first nor who was there, if anyone, when I was born. When I was older she told me that first off people weren't too nice. I always called her Cecilly, too, by the way—never knew her as anything else.

"But she had the gift you see? Planted out herbs and made tonics and potions and poultices for every which thing, and she could find underground water anywhere 'cept our place with these two bent up old wire coat hangers. Had this pack of cards and people'd come and she'd shoo me off to play while she'd tell 'em things private.

"Even as early as I can remember there was always somebody coming or going. Thing was, no one ever hung around. All she really had, people-wise, was me. When she wasn't busy she would read to me or else teach me about the stuff in the garden. Some nights she'd take me walking way off from the house and we'd lie on the ground on our backs while she pointed out what group of stars meant what. I loved that."

The waitress brings the juices and I pay then and there. Brighid keeps hold of one of my hands.

"Was when I went to school that the trouble started," I continue when we're by ourselves again, unable to shut up like Brighid has cast some kind of enchantment on me or something.

"Kids'd call me a bastard and go on and on about me not having a father; call Cecilly a slut and a witch, like it was a dirty word. First fight I was only six—they kept happening 'til Cecilly took me out of school a year later. The school never did send any authorities 'round to make me go back.

"I'd asked her about a dad, but she wouldn't say much. 'He was just a man,' she'd say dismissively, without meaning to hurt my feelings. I'd asked her about being a witch. She laughed at that and said, 'Whatever . . .'

"So in the end I'd do my chores and Cecilly would teach me, always bringing home dozens of books from the library, and I really liked it 'cause she was always so happy and excited about the stuff—it was like we were exploring the world together. It was her'd loved the history and the myths and stuff—passed the passion on, I suppose."

"What did she look like Jack?" asked Brighid.

"Oh, long dark brown hair smelling of the garden." I recall, as the memory of her when she was younger rose up so strongly she might have been just a mist away.

"She had strange eyes though—different colors, one blue and one brown—always changing with her moods. She was short too Brighid— just a tad taller than you. She used to let her hair hang loose mostly, 'though occasionally she'd tuck it all up under a cap when she had a lot of manual work to do. And strong, too, never seeming to need anyone." I paused, thinking.

"She died from pneumonia. Got real sick that deep cold winter three years back. I did all the right tisanes just like she'd showed me but she just got worse. I even went so far as to ask her if I could get in the doctor, maybe get those antibiotics into her. She wouldn't have it. 'Time I died,' she'd said. And did.

"When I was straightening away her stuff after I'd got her buried . . ."

Brighid interrupted me. "Where's she buried Jack?"

I smiled as I recalled. "A few miles south of here the land climbs up into the hills. We went there lots once we'd discovered it. Deep in there's this big slab of stone maybe twenty foot high and kinda up on its end. We'd always go there. Cecilly never had a problem leaving the set paths to go searching for the wild herbs, as they're always best. Right near that big slab of stone there's a pool that we used to cool our feet in on the hot days. It was spring-fed and never seemed to me to have a bottom. Wouldn't swim there. Buried her there.

"Anyway, when I was straightening up all her stuff, packing away most of it, I found a big old box that she had hidden away in back of the wardrobe. It had a lot of her memories in it. Photos of people I didn't know—old photos, some *really* old. Some old jewelry, the deed for the farm—never knew when, let alone how, she'd managed that. Never realized that we owned the place—and . . ."

I pause to look at Brighid. Why not? I say to myself.

". . . and a book of spells." Her eyebrows go up but that's about all. "And a letter that said Jack on the envelope.

"I remember that I was afraid to open that letter, don't know to this day why. I left it on the kitchen table for a whole week before I read it. I was angry for months after—and scared that maybe she'd been crazy all along and that I hadn't known it because I didn't know any better.

"In the letter she told me that she loved me and always would; that I wasn't supposed to get the letter 'til after she'd died in case I wouldn't love her anymore. Felt it was important, blah blah. She wrote in it that my father hadn't been a human; that she'd loved him but that he lived in an entirely other world and that he couldn't cross between like she could and that he'd been sad that he could never touch me or know me—his own child—and that she'd have to do all his loving and teaching *for* him. Said he was a man of the sídhe. Said he'd told her that someday he'd find a way . . ."

I stopped when Brighid took a huge deep breath. I'm rambling. "Sorry . . ." I say.

She's been looking down all throughout. She looks up now and her eyes are as smiling as her mouth, "That answers that then, doesn't it?" she says and kisses me fair on the lips.

I feel the blood rush to my face. And it's like perfect timing or something because the others have spotted us and are whooping and hollering on their way over to the table.

"Got it!" says Annis, all grins.

"Me too," says Brighid. I'm about to ask her what she means when we all hear it. Distant thunder.

Rowan joins us a few minutes later, all loaded with fresh supplies. We pile ourselves and the rest into the truck just as the strong smell of ozone wafts on the rising breeze.

It starts raining on the drive home.

The journey ends.

Take time to recover before continuing the ritual.

Take up the consecrated wine, sprinkle a little onto the food, and drink from the chalice. If there is another or others with you, share with them.

Light the wood in the brazier or fireplace with the altar-candle, saying:

> *I light the Beacon that lights the World*
> *The Seasons change, the Flowering of Life*
> *I honor my ancient inheritance—*
> *The freedom to Dance the draíocht*
> *With all who Dance to the Piper!*

To complete the Rite, raise the staff aloft and say:

> *Blessings be on Forest and on Field*
> *I call Blessed the Darkness as I call Blessed the Light!*

I call on the Déithe to reclaim the Lands
In the name of N . . . (name the Déithe),
By Mórrigan and all her Daughters—
By Earth, by Sky, by Sea
By the Sacred Law of Three!

Complete the ritual by farewelling the guardians and reversing the Circle as you've done before. Put away all ritual things and write any appropriate notes, then party.

The Ritual of the Midsummer Solstice: Meán Samhraidh
Requirements for the Ritual
You will need the usual things, plus a consecrated oil of storax, amber, and oakmoss; incense of sandalwood; oil of nightqueen; seasonal festive food; a fireplace or brazier. Gather deadwood to burn in the brazier or fireplace.

Set up for the ritual in the usual manner, and bathe with intent of purification.

When you are ready you will seat yourself before the altar, light the altar candle and the incense, and center yourself by using four-fold breathing leading to a soft, humming chant.

Use your staff to cast a Circle about yourself, saying:

O Circle of draíocht, outside of time,
keep all within and all without
and forge a barrier between them.
I seek to journey beyond the Veil.
Be ye cast in the names of N . . . (the Lady and Lord),
By Earth, by Sky, by Sea!

Using your wand and athame, invoke the guardians of the Four Gates.

Go to the altar and refuel the incense. Be still. Use whatever technique you have been practicing to prepare for the journey.

Listen to the Legend of the Summer Solstice, personalizing with all the characters in the story, for the entirety.

When you have done so, and can feel the Déithe within yourself, you'll continue the ritual to its conclusion.

The journey into Mythos is as follows:

The Solstice of Midsummer

I see a dark sail on the horizon
Set under a black cloud that hides the sun . . .

—Jethro Tull, from "Broadsword"

The bus chugs over the crest of the hill and we look down over the splendor of the bay.

"What a vision," I whisper to Hunter.

I slow the bus enough to drink in the sight. The sea in the distance is all whitecaps and dark blue water leading onto a long crescent of beach, the town right down close to the shore. The bay curves around like a big *U,* the hills hung with morning mist off to the left and the headland to the right dotted with all the headstones reflecting the early sunlight where the salt-spray had damped them during the night.

I crank the bus into low gear for the steep decline as a two-train semi barrels past me in the outside lane, causing the bus to take a sideways lurch toward the guard rail. Hate those things, I think.

Hunter's up front with me, with Robin belted into his lap playing some kind of finger game. The others are in back.

"Hey, come take a look!" I yell, and they all crowd up close for the big panorama.

"How you doing, Willie?" asks Jack. "Is it far now? Do you want me to take the wheel for a while?"

"Nah—be there in ten minutes as the crow flies," I reply grinning. Hunter chuckles at me as he passes Robin back to whoever will take him. He stretches in the seat.

"Home," he says softly.

The forest out back of the bay is the place of the summer gathering. A whole year's been spent in some really lousy destinations, playing some good gigs and some terrible, gathering the Lost along the way.

We found three of the Lost people this year—Rowan and Jack and Gypsy. Rowan and Black Annis (she's the one Jack insists on calling parrot-girl even though she's changed the color of her hair maybe five times since he met her—it's pink for the gathering) are an item. Jack still hasn't made the move on Brighid, though I'm not surprised—she's a pretty formidable babe.

And Gypsy? She worked at the cafe in the town near where we stayed last. Brighid had met her for just a brief moment the first morning in the town but she hadn't picked her 'cause Brighid had apparently been distracted by Jack at the time. We noticed her at the gig that night though. She'd been up front, dancing through every set, ice-white hair flying around her head as she let loose. Couldn't miss her really—she was the only person in the pub game enough to get on the dance floor.

Turns out she'd been a blow-in from the city and had landed the waitress job right off as the woman before her had only just left to have a baby. You wouldn't think to look at her that she'd be so deep down dark angry. Happens a lot, though, when the magic's strong in a person—they never do fit in with the surface world.

I cruise the bus down the main street of town. The sidewalks on both sides of the road are already crowded with tourists. Can spot a few of the folk among them—seems more are out and about than last year.

It's a bit easier here than most places we go. There are so many rainbow people and hippies and mystics and musicians and dreamers that already live here or else in the hills around the bay that the authorities don't pay us too much attention. We occasionally get searched for dope or guns—either that or they try to find something to give us a hard time over, but it's not like some places.

Jack's right up behind me leaning on the back of mine and Hunter's seats, staring and mumbling as he takes it all in. We got a bumper crop out of Jack's patch while we were at his place, and there was a bit of a frenzy getting all the medicinals ground and pounded and steeped and bottled and jarred, but we've got a pretty impressive load of lotions and potions on board—enough to share out at the gathering—and plenty of still-fresh produce, so we won't have to buy much, if anything.

Trevor stayed at Jack's place this year to keep the place going. He loves chickens and they took to him like Jack didn't exist anymore. Got to find ourselves another bodhrán player though. Still, I figure there'll be a stray or two at the fair.

Out the other side of town a way, we turn off onto the dirt track. We follow behind a big old blue car that's loaded with the folk. They're leaning out the windows calling and laughing as we eat their dust. That's okay, I think to myself, you can wait.

Hunter reaches over and pulls one of my plaits. "I can hear you thinking, Willie. Be nice," he grins. I smile back, sure of myself.

The battle of champions takes place every year at the gathering and I've been training pretty hard, doing the run to town from Jack's place over the roughest terrain I could find, and fighting with Hunter, who's really my only challenge among the band members.

The battle's got three categories—the run, the one-on-one staff fight, and the best filíocht. For the last three years Sheila ní Dubh has won the best poet and I'm nowhere near her league, and as far back as anyone can remember no one's ever beaten Hunter with the staff—but I intend to make a good second. The run's up for grabs.

I slow down as we pass through the wide gate and rattle over the cattle-grid on the last leg of the journey, and drive along a couple of hundred yards to where the forest opens out onto a huge clearing. Not many here yet so we get to pick a good spot to park the bus. I maneuver the thing into a pocket of deep shade 'cause by the time the sun's at mid-morning, it's going to be a scorcher.

Robert and Shauna, the custodians of this place, see us from where they're helping some guys to put up the big main marquee and come slowly over to greet us.

"By my Lady, Robert's looking old!" I say to Hunter as we set up camp, the others of the band bringing bits and pieces out of the bus.

Mate and Jessie start barking a warning, but Hunter looks in the dogs' direction. That shuts them up!

Robert's an O'Neill and Shauna's his good wife. His ancestors have been settled in this area since the time of the first crossing when most of us left the homeland due to the Troubles. An O'Neill, way back, decided that none of the family would partake of the Quicken Brew and none of them, to my knowledge, ever have. So they've lived and died quite contentedly, passing down the generations the task of hosting the gatherings—and keeping the secret.

They never get really personal with any of us—that's to save us the sadness, I figure. Love them for it.

Robert comes up to Hunter and does his little bow thing, just like they always do, saying "Fáilte, m'Lord," and they go off together to talk the news of the area so that Hunter can pass on anything significant to the rest of us and we can get word out if there's likely to be trouble.

Cars and vans keep coming all morning. People're erecting shelters and stalls to sell their stuff or whatever, and making little homes all over the clearing. I had to laugh, I suppose, when Rowan said to me, "They just look like anybody else, only weirder," as though he was expecting us to be the only normal-looking ones.

Today's just for setting up and playing music and getting to know each other again, for hearing the tales of the journeys and for meeting the special people that we've gathered along the way and who are prepared to work in with us. To find out which of them will take the Quicken Brew, once they know the danger.

Puck and Rowan and Gypsy and Jack have already been told. Jack's not sure he wants that kind of responsibility, even feeling like he does for Brighid. There's no way that Puck's not going to partake—like she and Hunter aren't going to love each other as far into the future as I can imagine! Rowan and Gypsy are in for the long ride, they've said already.

Oh, about Jack. When Robin was born we'd been sure he'd been the first of the half-kind. Hadn't known there'd been some rogue fairy out there making out with a witch in the backwater!

Brighid hates it when I use the *f* word. Can never get over the joke though—about having little wings and all. Cried myself to sleep the first time I heard what they'd turned us into for the sake of killing us off in people's minds. What? Did some freak figure we'd just go away after that? Still—got so I could see the funny side.

Hunter strides over to us looking grim. He sits down on the ground indicating for the rest of us to join him. There's a dark haze of worry all around him. He indicates for Brighid to sit to his left and Puck to his right. Oh, oh, I think, as the rest of us sit.

"Would you three mind not staying?" he asks, looking first at Gypsy, then Rowan, then Jack. Uh, oh, I think again, more and more alert. They leave us goodheartedly enough, but I can hear them wondering.

"There's been a fire," Hunter begins. "Kate O'Neill and her husband and their kids." Alarm bells.

"Bad?" asks Brighid, shock registering on her face.

"All dead," replies Hunter.

"But what about . . ." I begin.

"Stop," says Hunter, "I've got more." We wait. "It looks as though it was deliberate."

Confusion.

"*Why?*" asks Puck.

"Robert and Shauna are devastated," continues Hunter, his voice dark, his eyes like black coals as he looks around at all of us.

The penny drops. Kate and her children were the only living descendants of this branch of the O'Neills—the Guardians. Robert and Shauna are too old to take the Quicken Brew—it'd kill 'em even before their time.

End of the line.

"Who'd *do* this?" says Brighid.

"Well it's not because of the secret unless that husband of hers let it out," says Hunter.

"Did he know?" asks Puck, not fully up-to-date on the subject.

"He had to know. Kate's job is to raise the kids up to take it on will-ingly. Since they were born, Kate's brought them to every gathering so they could get used to us. Owen never came but he would've known. Robert's figured he's been trouble all along. Too fond of the drink—always been a worry."

Brighid's in tears. "They were just babies," she whispers. Kate's children were three and five years old this turning of the wheel.

"Well right now, whoever did this thing is still a mystery. Robert says the cops haven't got a clue. There were petrol drums that didn't belong there dumped at the scene and they've been sent off for DNA tests," con-tinued Hunter.

Silence.

"The gatherings . . ." says Matt.

"We'll have to wait 'til everyone's arrived," says Hunter. "Rowan and the others don't need to have their heads confused with any of this, okay? They need to be really cool for the ceremony. No one's to upset them, understood?" We all agree.

I just sit there thunderstruck. If we can't have the gatherings we'll be lost again. It took us hundreds of years to get over the inquisition. They were the worst years ever since the Christians took the old ways away from the land in the first place. Some of us actually died from the terror—the deepest sadness and despair is the only thing that can actually destroy the folk.

I shook myself. Don't go there, I think, coming out of that memory as quick as possible. Someone'll figure something out. Right now I need a run. A long run.

Hunter's nowhere.

I've been around all the fires asking after him. And where's Brighid?

The folk all gathered late afternoon to talk about the problem. Robert had been asked to attend and he'd filled in a few gaps that he hadn't told

Hunter earlier, one of which was that the cops hadn't been sure if Owen, Kate's husband, had even been in the house at the time. The house was over a hundred years old; a two-story wooden place that's gone up like matchsticks. The bodies inside weren't terribly recognizable when forensics had turned up. They'd been sure of the remains of Kate and the kids but if Owen *had* been there it's possible he'd been in a different part of the house and had been incinerated. If he hadn't? Well, no one's seen him since.

The meeting had broken up when the first of the Great Fires was due to be lit to mark the opening of the gathering.

It was dusk.

There'd been no resolution.

Everybody had lightened up once the first fire was lit—we had two more days to think of a solution and Robert, after all, could live for several more gatherings so no one seemed to think the dilemma was an immediate threat.

Bands had played into the night and people had danced and feasted and abandoned themselves to each other. Matt came up with a temporary bodhrán player named Alan, who was one of the Lost and hadn't got a foot in the door with any of the established bands—he'd been busting to play. Alan's a great guy—been playing with folk bands up and down the west coast for years now, never settling, as is common.

Fianna played the last set of the night and we rocked the house (as we do!). There was me on fiddle, Matt on the uilleann pipes and both the low whistle and the high whistle, Annis moved between accordion and the harp and backed up Puck—who does guitar—on vocals, and, of course, Alan was on the bodhrán.

We'd packed up and were having a dram. Puck had taken Robin back from Rowan, who'd been dancing him in his arms for most of the night, and had gone off looking for Hunter.

She hadn't found him, nor Brighid either.

What's going on?

"If he doesn't want to be found," says Puck, "then he won't be found—you know that Willie."

Still, it's strange for him to go off and not say a word to anyone.

Yeah, I know it, Puck—got a weird feeling, is all, I think to myself, not wanting to worry her unduly.

Jack comes over to where we're sitting 'round the hearthfire next to the bus.

"I found Brighid," he begins, "but she wants to be left alone to be with the land. She said Hunter borrowed Hugh Taylor's car and took off while the bands were playing."

Such a very weird feeling.

"I'm going to find him." I say, standing. Puck's looking at me, her look loaded with unspoken concern.

"You heard what Puck said," pipes up Annis.

"Don't care." No argument.

The last car in was John Finch's. His band's camped right near the track so I go over and ask if I can use his wheels for a while.

"Well I'm not going anywhere," he slurs, several Guinness's the merrier. "Keys are in it," and he returns his attention to his companions.

I've got a gut feeling he's gone out to Kate's place. It's a half-hour drive from when I leave the track and get on the main road. I drive.

I park the car on the track side of the police cordon tape and pass under it and up to the mess. All that's left is the chimney, a lot of cold blackened timber, ash, and iron roofing that's scattered around. The garden shed's still standing though. I've got to fight not to lose it, but my eyes are stinging.

The place stinks. Fear, horror, something unclean I can't quite get— but I can also smell that Hunter's been here already, and gone.

My heart's beating in my throat. Something really bad has happened here—that's the unclean thing that's up my nose. It's worse closer to the shed.

Sit. Touch the earth. Don't know what it was other than the fire. Something. I get myself calm.

"Where's Hunter?" I summon. *"Headland."* I hear it as quick as that.

"Blessings," I say aloud to the earth and the forest around me.

The moon's high overhead, near full. Wind's soft off the ocean as I walk along the cliff-edge with the buried dead to my right.

I see the silhouette of Hunter's bulk right over at the farthest point of the headland. I wander over, fox-wary, and sit down beside him as casually as I can, knowing that my interference could easily backfire.

I look out of the corner of my eye and can see his jaw clench and unclench. I don't want to initiate a conversation with him—known him a long time and when the dark man gets dark you don't push him. And it's been a while since I've sensed him this dark.

Eventually he rolls his head around to loosen up some stiffness. He's still looking out to sea.

"It was him," he says softly.

"Who?" I ask.

"Owen," he answers.

"You sure?"

"Dead sure," he replies.

"What happens now?" I ask, already knowing where this is going.

"These people have been our allies—our friends—all the way back," he says very quietly.

He stretches and stands and holds out a hand to pull me up. "First we're gonna celebrate the Turning," he says, "and then I'm going to find him.

"We get back to the camp and you tell Black Annis I got her things outta the shed. Tell her I want a word. I need to be with Puck right now," and he strides off toward the car park.

Uh, oh, I think.

As if I didn't know.

Daybreak and there's a knock on the side of the bus that wakes everybody with its insistence. Annis goes and opens it. It's Shauna.

"Sorry to wake you," she says, "but it's important. It's Robert . . ."

"Can you wait a minute Shauna," calls Hunter, pulling his pants on.

"I'll be lighting your hearthfire, Lord," she calls. Annis chortles at the title.

Shauna's sitting beside a stoic-looking Robert, who's got his hands clamped together in his lap, sitting up straight and dressed like he's going to court. The fire's burning brightly and Shauna's put a kettle on to boil.

Robin crawls over to Rowan, his current favorite, and Rowan proceeds to distract him.

Puck sits down beside Hunter and Robert stands.

"I have something to say to you all," he stutters, looking down at his feet. "Relax, Robert," says Shauna.

"Yeah chill, Robert," pipes Annis.

"We want to take the Quicken Berry Brew," says Robert.

"You . . ." begins Hunter.

"I'm sorry to interrupt you Lord, but please . . ." whispers Robert.

"Please hear him out, Lord," says Shauna. "We've discussed this at great length and have already made plans."

"I'm listening," Hunter replies gravely.

"I've made up my mind," he begins. "All of you have been our blessing right back to when we were high kings and beyond. A branch of the O'Neills have always guarded the secret, and since the crossing it's been our honor—no, our *life*—to keep a piece of the land sacred for both our people.

"Now all that's in jeopardy, and me and mine," he looks lovingly at Shauna, "have got two choices—bear it in mind that we're going to die anyway without the second choice.

"First choice is to maybe have a few seasons left and then we die, with no O'Neill to keep the pact." Shauna cries softly into her handkerchief.

"Second choice is to take the Sacred Brew, despite the risk, because then we'd get the longevity we'd need to keep the lands for the gatherings, just like we always have. When we don't get any older, we can deal with the curious when the time comes—nobody takes much notice of old people anyway. Shauna won't let me do it without her, just in case I up and die on her." He looks at all the silent faces.

"And I've covered all the possible problems." He smiles at Hunter.

"Go on," says Hunter.

"I've booked Shauna and me on a flight to the old country already. We're due to get on the plane the day after the gathering concludes.

"If we die from the potion then we want you to just bury us here, where we love it—no fuss. If we live we'll take the holiday anyway. One way or the other the authorities won't know anything. We went to town yesterday and mentioned the trip to a few key locals. We told them that we're taking an extended tour and that we'd no idea when we'd be back—and due to our recent tragedy people understand our need to get away.

"We told them that we've had the title of the place put in a distant niece's name . . ." he nods at Puck, ". . . in case we decide to stay there."

"What are you doing, Robert!" says Puck.

"You're the only one we know among the folk who's like us. You've got a past and you were the only one of the Lost that we know well enough to write out details on the transfer," he continues. "Authorities'd check up on any of the rest of you and find out you've got no past—no records—that'd stand up under scrutiny. That could be trouble for you."

"I'm taking the brew tonight," says Puck.

"They won't know that," states Robert emphatically. "Please, just give us a go . . ."

"You know the risk," says Hunter, standing. "So be it," and he reaches over to shake Robert and Shauna's hands.

We held the challenges that afternoon. I didn't win the run but I came second to Seamus the Red, which is pretty good. Hunter chose not to compete, which only means that no one else gets a go at his title until next year. I did bloody badly at the staff—distracted I suppose.

Sheila won the filíocht challenge *again*—I don't believe it!

Rowan and Puck and Gypsy and the other six Lost people took the Brew as the sun set, and made it through to begin a life of a long, long time.

Jack refused, saying maybe next time to Brighid, who finally came back from wherever in the draíocht that she'd gone since the meeting. I figure she knows the pattern—she's got that look in her eyes.

I passed on the message to Annis, who just smiled.

Robert and Shauna died from the Brew. Died quietly journeying the Otherworld, smiles on their faces as they traveled beyond our reach.

The end of a line of great kings. The end of the Guardians.

Everybody gathered on the third day, when we put them into the earth, to bid them fair skies and a strong wind at their backs on the journey into the West.

No one's certain about the future.

Hunter never said a word to anyone else about what he'd told me.

On the bus, back on the highway—and it's pretty late so there's no traffic—Jack's at the wheel with Matt playing the low whistle softly in the seat beside him.

I'm trying to get to sleep like most of the rest of our company. Brighid and Hunter are the only ones back here who are still sitting up. They haven't talked for days.

"I know it all," I overhear Brighid say quietly to the big man.

"So . . ." he replies quietly.

"Hmm," she sighs, "I know where this is going. I know it all too well."

The journey ends.

Take the time to recover before proceeding.

Take up the consecrated wine, sprinkle a little onto the food, and drink from the chalice. If there is another or others with you, share with them.

Light the wood in the brazier or fireplace with the altar-candle, saying:

I light the Beacon that lights the World
The Fruit that hides the future's Seed is the food of life and death,
I honor my ancient inheritance—
The freedom to Dance the draíocht
With all who Dance to the Piper!

To complete the Rite, raise the staff aloft and say:

Blessings be on Forest and on Field
I call Blessed the Darkness as I call Blessed the Light!
I call on the Déithe to reclaim the Lands

> *In the name of N . . . (name the Déithe),*
> *By Mórrigan and all her Daughters—*
> *By Earth, by Sky, by Sea*
> *By the Sacred Law of Three!*

Complete the ritual by farewelling the guardians and reversing the Circle as you've done before. Put away all ritual things and write any appropriate notes, then party.

The Ritual of the Autumn Equinox: *Meán Fómhair*
Requirements for the Ritual

You will need the usual things, plus a consecrated oil of storax, amber, and oakmoss; incense of sandalwood; oil of nightqueen; seasonal festive food; a fireplace or brazier. Gather deadwood to burn during the ritual.

Set up for the ritual in the usual manner, and bathe with intent of purification.

When you are ready you will seat yourself before the altar, light the altar candle and the incense, and center yourself by using four-fold breathing leading to a soft, humming chant.

Use your staff to cast a Circle about yourself, saying:

> *O Circle of draíocht, outside of time, keep all within and all without*
> *and forge a barrier between them.*
> *I seek to journey beyond the Veil.*
> *Be ye cast in the names of N . . . (the Lady and Lord),*
> *By Earth, By Sky, By Sea!*

Using your wand and athame, invoke the guardians of the Four Gates.

Go to the altar and refuel the incense. Be still. Use whatever technique you have been practicing to prepare for the journey.

Listen to the Legend of the Autumn Equinox, personalizing with all the characters in the story, for the entirety.

When you have done so, and can feel the Déithe within yourself, you'll continue the ritual to its conclusion.

The journey into Mythos is as follows:

Autumn Equinox

> Could you get behind a slow marching band?
> And join together in the passing
> of all we shared through yesterdays
> in sorrows neverlasting.

—Jethro Tull, from "Slow Marching Band"

It seems a long time since summer, so much has happened. I'd never thought that life could have gotten any more complicated than before I joined up with the Fianna. Still, it's done now.

Hunter says we'll be going back to the city before the winter and I guess I'm dreading it—no fond memories there. But that's the way of it. The band's gotta go where the work is and there are others lost besides me.

I love these people. Took me in without knowing anything about me. 'Least not anything I told them anyway.

Rowan found us this cottage and it's a good place. I'm always sensing the draíocht strongest in the autumn and the land here's alive with it.

I remember when we were driving up here and I commented on the thick fog that was making visibility on the road near impossible.

"Not fog," Hunter had said softly from the driver's seat beside me.

"Is s-so!" I'd argued.

"Not fog!" yelled Rowan from the back with the others. Annis had laughed and I'd sat brooding all scrunched up in my seat. She'd come up behind me and ruffled my hair and told me not to be so touchy.

The bus had labored at the steep climb and I remember wondering if it was going to make it all the way up the mountain to this mystery place that Rowan was so excited about. And I thought they'd been mucking me around about the fog till we drove right up through it.

Hunter had stopped the bus at a roadhouse, right in front of a tourist lookout, for coffee and a snack. We'd all clambered out into the hazy afternoon sunlight and I was struck by the crisp bite in the air—at how clean it was.

I wandered to the men's room down the side of the petrol outlet to relieve myself and splash water on my face, then I headed over to the lookout. Oh wow!

We were suspended on the brink of a sheer dropoff and we were up above the cloud! Great plumes, like towers, rose from the lazy white thickness below me. I leaned over the guardrail and got that weird sensation that I get in really high places. I discovered later that the cliff goes down thousands of feet to the valley below where the rapids tumble through gorges covered with moss and bracken and ancient trees.

We arrived at the cottage about a half hour after the pit stop. We'd passed through a little village that looked like it had come right out of "Ye Olde Merrie" except for the few tourist shops and McDonalds.

We're down at the very end of Baton Lane, last place before the drop, just across the forest from the dairy. The drive in is along a track crowded on either side with huge pines and maples and silver birch, the last two doing their amazing red and gold color thing. I had the window rolled right down on the way in and the whole place smelled like heaven.

The cottage has got the power on to the house but the toilet's out back in a weather-beaten cloister with a makeshift door, and the bathroom is off the side of the house, like someone forgot it when they originally built the place. It's got a big old enamel iron bath but no shower, and you have to fire up a wood-chip stove to heat the water.

We've got verandas all around the house and you can't get to any of the bedrooms from the inside—got to come out the kitchen and walk around the veranda. The heart of the cottage is that kitchen but the living room's its soul—it's in the center of every room, with the inner walls of the three bedrooms backing onto it, the fourth wall gracing an enormous fireplace that shares its chimney, and a doorway, with the kitchen. We keep the fire burning in there all day and all night against the mountain chill—it keeps the bedrooms warm as well. (I guess if I'm going to be somewhere cold this time of year then here's the best place ever.)

The gigs up here are terrific. Seems like everyone from anywhere around the mountain, or from down in the valley, has come to dance and drink while we play. Wally's the owner of the pub and he's been like Mr. Red Carpet since we tried out for him. Food and drinks have all been on the house each night we've played. The place has been packed and there hasn't been one rude comment about the way we look.

I've played with lots of bands over time and some of them have been really good, but they were never family and they didn't have the draíocht and I'd never stopped yearning to belong.

I don't know if I'll be with Fianna once we join Trevor next spring but Willie's pretty certain that two bodhrán players are going to be better than one. "And all that aside," he'd said mischievously, "who else'd have you?" So my heart's not breaking at the prospect of having to leave.

I've talked for hours—days—with Brighid, about what she calls "the gift" and how to work with it. Finally.

See since I was a boy I've seen what I figured were ghosts. Seen 'em everywhere. And it seems I spent most of my childhood thinking this was normal.

I remember when I was about five or six, something like that, having a conversation with this woman whose name was Helen. My mother hadn't long been with her new boyfriend Jeff and she was pregnant with Tracy already but they'd decided not to cancel the summer holiday that we'd booked earlier.

We were staying in this old beachside house that we'd rented for two weeks. I was out in the yard when Helen had come out the back door and over to where I was lying on my stomach watching lizards fighting like real dinosaurs. She'd said it was nice that we'd come to stay with her; that she was on her own the rest of the year until the summer visitors came. She'd thought her son Rick must have made the arrangements—she never sees him anymore and she's sad about that.

We were chatting about all the things I could do during the holidays when my mother came out from the house and asked me who I thought I was talking to.

"This is Helen," I introduced. Mum just kinda looked at me funny and ignored Helen and told me to come inside for lunch. I told Helen I'd maybe see to her soon. She just smiled at me and looked over to my mother's receding back.

Later that night I overheard my mother talking to her boyfriend and telling him that I had an imaginary friend.

I was really confused.

Over the years there were hundreds of them and I realized that no one else besides me could see or hear them. That was kinda scary but I figured that everybody's different and that other people must see other things that I couldn't see. Some of the ghosts were nice and some were horrible, and some were really sad or scared. Each of them had a story to tell.

By the time I was twelve years old my mother had me to a psychiatrist and he'd asked me lots of questions—mostly stupid—about how I'd felt when my dad left, as if I could remember, and about my mother and her boyfriend and Tracy, my little sister. I told him they were cool. Everything was cool. No problem. Nothing wrong. Nothing bothering me. He never shut up looking to find shit. Asked lots of questions about the people I "thought" I saw.

"N-no," I'd said stammering. None of his business. I lied about them because I knew he was trouble. Prescribed these pills I was supposed to take to make the ghosts go away and make me feel better, like I didn't feel fine—just crowded.

Well, I took the pills for a while just to get everybody off my back. They didn't do anything and I was still getting the people coming and still hearing their stories, so in the end I just pretended to take the pills to make my mother happy and so I wouldn't have to see that stupid doctor anymore.

And I stopped talking so I wouldn't stutter anymore. Hardly said anything other than "yes," "no," "please," "thank you," "maybe," and "yeah okay," for about a year.

Then my mother's best friend from when she was at school came to visit.

Julie.

She'd been living abroad and studying music the last few years. That first night she stayed she'd played a tape of a band called The Chieftains.

My whole world stopped. I asked her to play it again when the tape finished, and again when it finished the second time. She'd laughed that big open-mouthed laugh that I'll love 'til the day, sometime in the ancient future, when I maybe die.

I think I fell in love for the first time. She had this crop of short, fire-engine red hair and eyes like forests and a cute mouth with an overbite. She was all dance and song and laughter.

She stayed a week and played me variations of the same kind of music, and talked about the lyrics and the style and the instruments. She had a tin whistle and a flute and a bodhrán.

Then, after she left—and me with a broken heart—I fell in love again. With poetry and the legends of Fionn MacCumhaill and the tales of the Red Branch and the mysteries of Morrígan and Macha and Badb, with Breo-saight, who some call Brighid, and the high kings of Teamhair, and the Tuatha dé Danann and the music—oh, the music!

I wrote to Julie, like she was my religion, for the whole of the following year and then, one day just like today, but windier and city, this stranger comes to our door.

My mother answers the knock and there's this tall, lean guy with black hair all shaven across the front of his head and braided everywhere else, pale skin, gray eyes, all dressed in black, with a little silver harp earring hanging from one ear.

My mother's all suspicious until he tells her that Julie sent him to me.

Mum shows him into the apartment, still wary. He comes right on over toward where I'm sitting with my book abandoned, all curiosity at my visitor. I stand up as he approaches and he holds out his empty hand and shakes mine vigorously.

"You staying around here?" asks my mother.

"Not far," he replies.

"You here for long?" she asks.

"I'm here for Alan," he answers, grinning.

"Hmm," she says. "Can I get you something?"

"Water?" he says.

"Well, I'll be right back." She sounds really on edge when all *I* am is excited.

He's got this big round package tucked in his other arm. We sit on the floor and he holds it out to me.

"Julie sent you this," he says. I touch the brown paper wrapper with reverence.

"Well open it, sunshine!" he laughs.

I undo the string, already knowing from the shape of it what's inside.

Raven comes around just on twilight each night. He brings his own bodhrán with him and teaches me. He's really patient 'cause I figure I'm never going to get the hang of it and 'cause every time I go to ask a question my stutter's really bad. He tells me I'm doing fine.

Some nights the room's crammed with ghosts but they're mostly there to listen. I work pretty hard at not looking at them but Raven pipes up with "It's like bloody Grand Central Station in here, boy!"

"You can see 'em?" I ask, incredulous.

"Nah, just sense 'em, sunshine," and he simply continues the lesson.

He's the one that starts telling me about the magic. He calls it the *draíocht*.

Then one night after several weeks he doesn't come. That's okay, I guess.

But then the next night he doesn't show up either, and I'm really scared I've lost my only friend.

The following day the post drops off a thick brown envelope with my name on it, postmarked from somewhere not here. I get that kinda sick feeling when I touch it, knowing it's from him and knowing I'm not going to be happy about it.

Inside is a beat-up thin stack of papers stapled together with Thomas the Rymer written on the cover and a note from Raven saying sorry he didn't get to explain but that we'd meet up again down the track.

My mother came into my room. I was fighting hard not to cry but she said it was a good thing really 'cause he'd been such a weirdo and she'd never trusted him and that she and Jeff had thought about not letting him come anymore anyway as they were always on edge when he was around, especially with the two of us up here on our own together.

That night I shoved a few things into my backpack, put Thomas the Rymer into my coat pocket and the bodhrán into its cloth bag, and climbed out of the window. I left my mother a note that was quite polite really, explaining that I just couldn't do it the way people seemed to think I should.

I've never been back, but I phoned occasionally until one time I called and they'd moved and now I don't know where they are anyway.

I took to living off the streets. For a while I stayed in the squats but I was mostly freaked out by the people who lived there and wasn't liking the way things got after dark. Place was full of ghosts, mostly in such a state of tragedy that I was suffocated by them. So I made myself quite a good shelter in the park down by the memorial. I started busking during the day.

I eventually discovered the municipal library and used to spend hours there reading everything from myths and legends and books on paranormal phenomenon and poetry to witchcraft and other books that were maybe about the draíocht. The witchcraft stuff was the most familiar—like all these people here and now working with the spirits of the land and honoring the legends and the old ways and the sky and the waters and a god and a goddess that are living things and not some pasty dead judgment like we used to get fed when I was in school. I figured I was one of them and started doing my own secret rituals down under the bridge by the canal.

Pat at the library used to lock up after me whenever I was there at closing time, which was most nights. In the end she let me stay and use the utilities room to bunk down in, telling me how much trouble she'd get into if I didn't do the right thing by her.

That summer I'd started using a deck of tarot to make a bit of extra money from the tourists. There was a market in the east end of town every Saturday and I'd spread out a cloth on the ground and try looking intensely mystical. I had a few people on the first day, out for a bit of a laugh and being really skeptical 'cause I was so young, but I brazened it out, stammer and all.

Thing was, each of them brought the shadow of their lives, or their own ghosts, with them, and so when I talked to the people I said a lot of stuff that I got from them, not the cards.

The weeks after that there was always this queue waiting to get to me. I didn't charge a lot of money but I was eating.

On weekdays I was busking with the bodhrán. Sometimes others'd join me with the fiddle or a whistle or a guitar and we'd do pretty well just jamming.

Then I met Riley Dougherty who'd stopped to listen. He had a pub down on the south side and said it was called Mary Dooly's Tavern and that lots of bands playing traditional folk music worked there Thursday and Saturday nights and that I ought to think about coming over and maybe getting in on some gigs.

So I did.

Always played filler though—tough to get in. Most bands were used to playing together and I was just too much used to being a loner to even consider the hard work of starting up my own combo.

The last Saturday before the Summer Solstice and we're almost finished with the first set when I see Raven over at the bar. He's grinning madly. Can't tell you how I got through that set without a mistake!

Came the break and I'm shoving people out of the way and grabbing him like a life raft and he's chuckling and hugging me back.

When I finally let go he sits back down on his stool and takes a gulp from his pint. "You've improved on the bloody drum, I see," he says with a twinkle in his eye.

"Where've you been!" I yell over the crowd.

"Doesn't matter," he replies casually. "What're you doing after the gig?"

"No plans," I answer, knowing I never really have any anyway.

"You feel like traveling?" he asks.

"Where to?"

"Meet up with some folk at a high summer gathering," he replies mysteriously.

I hear the *thuk, thuk* of the wood-splitter and figure Hunter and Matt are back from the forest with a load.

Brighid and Rowan are cutting up root vegetables to go into the oven for the feast later and Puck's outside brushing the honey and herb baste onto the wild goat that Hunter and Annis tracked down with Hunter's compound earlier in the day. Robin's sitting up on a chair beside me, "reading" to me, out of his little pop-up book, some story that's not written down.

Jack's gone off to look for wild mint to add to the greens and Willie's sitting up next to the stove playing his fiddle. Raven went off in the bus to get some mead and ale from the pub in town.

Since the Quicken Brew all my senses have honed. I can see farther, I can hear in a way I figure a hound might; touch is so much sweeter than it ever used to be; food's amazing—but the nose is the best bit. I walk out into the misty garden. Wood-smoke and roasting meat and damp undergrowth and old pine trees and the ancient rock that's all around the place. And nothing's ever smelled so good. And nothing's ever felt so right.

Brighid told me and the others where the Fianna are going after the feast tonight. They said they'd be taking us if we were willing (as if!). This'll be the first time I've traveled there outside of my imagination.

It's very late. The sky is huge and black and moonless, glittering with stars and frost. We're all out around the remnants of the feast and the fire's down to embers. Brighid lays out the offering of food for the creatures of the forest as Hunter and Puck share the last of the mead with the rest of us, and pour some to the earth in a blessing of the land.

Everyone waits, in quiet excitement, as Hunter raises the ancient horn to his lips . . .

The journey ends.

Take time to recover before continuing with the ritual.

When you light the brazier or the fireplace/pit, you will say:

> *I light the Beacon that lights the World*
> *The Seasons change, the Seeds of Life*
> *In honor of my ancient inheritance!*
> *In freedom to dance within the Earth,*
> *And upon the Earth, and above the Earth,*
> *with all who dance to the Piper!'*

To complete the Rite, raise the staff aloft and say:

> *The God of Light dwells enthroned*
> *Within the labyrinth of Future and Past.*
> *He dwells with the Dragon and the Lady of the Deep*
> *And there they guard the Circle*
> *By the Names of Artu, Lugh, Cernunnos, Bel, Herne*
> *By Mórrigan and all her Daughters—*
> *By Earth, by Sky, by Sea*
> *By the Sacred Law of Three!*

Complete the ritual by farewelling the guardians and reversing the Circle as you've done before. Put away all ritual things and write any appropriate notes, then party.

13   The Mórrigan

*When nature wants to make a man / to do the future's will /
when she tries with all her skill and she yearns with all her soul /
to create him large and whole / with what cunning she prepares him /
how she goads and never spares him / and in poverty begets him . . . /
how she often disappoints / whom she sacredly anoints . . .*

—Angela Morgan

Before continuing I would like to introduce you to the Déithe Mórrigan so that no one is under the illusion that this book denies the Lady.

The Mórrigan would have to have had the worst PR of just about any Déithe outside of the Christian devil. She is portrayed as a battle-savage demoness ripping at the flesh of fallen warriors; malevolent; a haglike figure who delighted in setting men at war.

The origins of the Morrígan seem to reach directly back to a megalithic matrilineal culture, and she was usually considered as tripartite—the face of birth and life and death.

The name "Mórrigan" is more aptly a title: Mór Rigan, which means "Great Queen," and she is the face of magic, sorcery, shapeshifting, prophecy, and the truth of the way life *really* is, with its blessings and its tragedies, life and death, and seeming unpredictability. In knowing her one takes off the rose-tinted glasses and sees what's to be seen without the frills; therefore, she is a great mentor despite the challenges that she sets, for experience is her deepest teaching, and how to deal with all situations in their context.

Later Celtic goddesses of sovereignty, such as the trio of Eire, Banba, and Fótla, also use magic in warfare, but they influence in that sphere of activity by means of magic and incantation rather than through physical strength.

In addition to being the champion of warriors in battle, the Mórrigan is significantly associated with fate, and she is said to appear before a death to guide the spirit to the Otherworld.

The Morrígan is an appropriate Déithe for strong, independent people, particularly witches who also train in the warrior arts.

At the time of the holocaust perpetuated by the Romans on the tribes of ancient Britain, Boudica was chieftain (and sorceress) of the Iceni, powerful enough to lead a revolt of united tribes against the invaders—that almost succeeded. Her Déithe was Andrasta, goddess of ravens and of battles—the Mórrigan by another name.

The Mórrigan, in the form of the raven (or crow) is a messenger, an oracle, and a muse. In legend she is said to have informed the Dagda of the landing place of the Fomorians, and so gave the Tuatha dé Danann the advantage prior to battle.

She sets out to confuse men through her human female representatives just to see if you can see through to her true face. I wonder at the legend of her advances to Cú Chulainn, which were spurned (for whatever reasons), leading to assault after assault in one guise after another (she's the very soul of shapeshifting) until he meets her in such a benevolent form—an old woman milking a cow—that he blesses her and so releases the geas between them.

The Mórrigan is an extremely draíochta (magical) Déithe, being considered the "foundation of sorcery" providing assistance magically, logistically, and environmentally in times of duress or trouble.

The Mórrigan, together with Brighid and Danu (Anu), form the land and the seasons and cycles of life in its infinitude of expressions, and it could also be said that each is the other, as is my understanding of her.

The Welsh tripartite equivalent: Arianhrod, Ceridwen, and Rhiannon.

14 The Union of Goddess and God

O lead me to the Silver Gate, the Moon Gate,
the places of the Shining Ones!

—Ly de Angeles, "In Nomini Mater Meum"

This ritual focuses on the importance of love (a thing no one can happily live without).

Mutual, intimate love has denied the Déithe of many of the world's traditional religions (with the exception of Hinduism), and, because adoration from the masses hardly constitutes a substitute, the Rite of Union is your way of honoring that intimacy.

Full Moon, the Rite of Union

Within your circle you will need a pentacle, an athame, a wand, a chalice, salt and water in separate containers, wine (within your cup), and five candles and candlesticks (one for your altar and the other four for the Elemental Gates). You will also need something with which to light the candles and the incense (and charcoal blocks), a book and a pen for logging your experience, and a dark cloth to cover your head if you're not wearing a hooded garment.

The ritual space is clean and in readiness, and everything is set up.

Bathe with intent, and oil your body.

Enter the space, light the altar-flame and the incense, and seat yourself before the altar. Begin with four-fold breathing, leading to a soft, humming chant until you are "centered" (leaving one world and entering another).

When you are ready, stand and take your athame, kiss the blade, and cast the Circle.

Summon the guardians of the Elemental Gates as previously, and light the candles with the altar candle to complete the Circle.

Return to your altar and replace the altar candle and the pentacle.

Take up the water in its container, concentrate, place the blade of your athame within it, and say softly:

Blessings be upon thee.

See the water being infused with draíocht from the blade.

When it is charged, replace it on the altar and take up the vessel of salt. Place the tip of your blade into it, concentrate, and say:

Blessings be upon thee.

Feel the salt being infused with draíocht. When it is charged you will add it to the water and stir them both together. Take some of it onto your finger and draw the pentagram of spirit on your forehead (self-blessing) before replacing the container on the altar.

Take up your chalice (the wine will already be in it) and place your athame blade therein. Contemplate the union (see appendix B: "As the Cup is to Woman . . . ?").

This is a draíocht of great reverence to Life.

Direct awareness from your blade into the wine.

Blessed be this Union
Blessed be Imramma
Blessed be the Déithe
Blessed be the draíocht
Blessed be N . . . (name the Lady and Lord).

Replace your athame upon the altar, raise the cup as a gesture of your understanding and alliance, and drink, in full understanding of what you do.

Replace the things on the altar, ascertain that the censer is still glowing, and refuel it with incense.

Having appropriate music will aid the intent of the rite. If you are a beginner (and this simple Esbat is aimed at the witch just starting out), then contemplation on what you consider significant and practicing your skills of visualization and focus will do to begin with. At the completion of your time within your sacred space, you will farewell the guardians, call back the draíocht of the Circle into your athame, and earth it.

> Especially, do not feign affection. Neither be cynical about love;
> for in the face of all aridity and disenchantment it is as perennial
> as the grass.
>
> —Max Ehrmann, "Desiderata"

15   The Four Fire Festivals

Seo an Tine Choisricthe!

—Translated from Irish Gaelic: "Behold the Sacred Fire!"

The Fire Festivals have their traditional associations, but to realize each fully you truly need to take into account where you live.

Tradition is one thing, but tradition that denies the "reality" of your own hearthland is pointless because the Fire Festivals are seasonal, earth-relevant celebrations, and *where* you live is how you celebrate.

Please note that whereas earlier in this book I have related, firstly, each association to the Northern Hemisphere, this section is focusing on the earth's seasons as we experience them, and are therefore biased by personal environment. Your work will require you to adjust your observations accordingly.

Deosil / Widdershins

There have been debates on this subject between the many branches of the "pagan" community for as far back as I can remember, and they mostly have very "logical" and intellectually appropriate arguments. The biggest (is this news?) has been about deosil/widdershins, and whether to cast a Circle clockwise or counterclockwise in the Southern Hemisphere.

To each his or her own, sure, but the fact of the matter is that as long as we've had a sun, a moon, or stars in the night sky, they've moved from horizon to horizon, in this part of the world, in a different direction from the Northern Hemisphere. Anti-clockwise.

Life would have been so much less complicated if the observers of the "natural world" who had attended the colonialists that invaded the South Pacific, Australia, and New Zealand had paid more attention and had invented a clock that goes seemingly backward.

So I'm going to describe to you how we celebrate the Fire Festivals here in Byron Bay, Australia, where the temperature rarely dips below 20°C, which is very different from the way we celebrated when we lived in the highlands of Victoria, where winter is remembered as sometimes dropping to -10°C in a cold year.

The reason I mention this is so that you can begin to *really* get in touch with where you live and the way you, personally, relate to your own tuath.

To do this is to undertake a one- to three-year study of observation to enable you to understand what occurs naturally in the seasons and cycles.

Aussie Style

The main thing that we do is party.

Each of the solstices and equinoxes and each of the Fire Festivals is a profound excuse for the coven and our circle of family and friends to get together (despite the fact that we're around each other most of the time anyway) and feast, play music, laugh, dance, love, and honor the turning of the wheel.

What is interesting when thinking about all of you who celebrate in the northern lands is that we are all very aware of our seasons being directly opposite yours but strangely similar in their extremes. When you are in the dead heart of the cold times in February, we're in the dead heart of searing heat—the grass is yellow and dead, burned by the sun, and hardly anyone can move because it's just so damn hot your feet get stuck to the asphalt if you attempt to cross the road barefoot, and staying out of doors too long can literally kill you.

Your Spring Equinox, which displays the first buds of new growth—an exquisite relief after the bone-numbing cold—gives us the wet season when, despite the days still being very hot, it rains for weeks and everything comes alive again. When we're in the middle of June the sun shines every day despite cold nights—your summer. So on go the comparisons. Kind of opposite but equal.

We're very aware of the traditions of our ancestors, and any and all ritual is reverential to them and all of the Déithe—we're their expression on the journey of Imramma—but we never forget the Big Picture.

Llughnassad

(Around February 2; August 1 in the Northern Hemisphere.)

The Season of the Red Dragonfly and Brown Snakes Mating.

We are very aware not to walk in long grass because when the brown snakes are in their mating season they are very aggressive. Australia is venomous. From coast to coast we probably have more creatures that bite, sting, and kill than any other populated land. Therefore we are mostly a little crazy.

Llughnassad is one time of the year when an outdoor fire (unenclosed) is not made, as this is also bushfire season, with most of the countryside tinder dry and the likelihood of water shortages a constant awareness.

The ritual itself might include a trek along the pathway that leads through dense rainforest to Protestor's Falls, where you can swim naked in the deep pool at the base of the falls and sun yourself straddling the moss-covered rock of the Forest God that protrudes from the center of the pool. Mmm!

Lugh: As with most of the Déithe of the Celtic pantheon, Lugh represents the fullness of life (including both love and the betrayal of love) and the transition of life, death, and rebirth. His symbol is the spear (represented in ritual as the staff and wand). The golden eagle is the totem of his death.

The staff and the wand are both very strong serpent symbols. Llugnassad is the time of the harvest of crops, fruit, and vegetables, representing the reaping. The significance of fire and death at this time on the wheel is very strong in this land, and Lugh is venerated simply because his persona as a strong solar Déithe and a lord of life and death is so very apt.

Effigies of twisted grasses or canes can be made to symbolize what needs to die upon the Llughnassad Fires (be nice! no politicians!), such things as old memories, harsh emotions, inappropriate attachments.

Samhain

(Around April 30; October 31 in the Northern Hemisphere.)

The End of the Wet Season—Carpet Snakes Enter the Ceilings.

New Year's Eve.

It would have rained day in, day out, for weeks by the time Samhain arrives. We've probably had a flood and most of the ground is still under water. The frogs are loud at night and the place is reeking of rotting vegetation.

When we light the fires on the night of Samhain it's as much to drive away the damp as to celebrate the eve of the new year.

An intense awareness of the fragility of life abounds, as does the relief everyone's feeling that the hot days are in decline . . . but many of us who live here are very attuned to the tropics, so that even with the deepening cool we think of winter with regret at summer's passing.

In the deep throes of autumn the air is full of the smells of woodsmoke . . . and the mozzies are demonic. They breed in every pot lid, swamp, water tank, every vessel that the neglectful forgot to overturn, and Ross River fever is feared all across the northern rivers—one bite and the next three years of your life is spent in a battle of exhaustion and pain.

Every second person has suffered tropical ulcers or head lice or some form of fungus or other. Around here people talk about such things with a rakish air of "So what?"

For us, honoring all that has ever lived is what Samhain is all about. This is the time of year when the many people that the land has rejected leave the area, and if anyone is going to move house this is when they do so because most of the tourists and transients have gone and the local people stand a chance of reclaiming their tuath from the invaders.

And always there's Willie and the Wild Zinnias summoning the dancers to the floor at the Railway pub with fires lit in the barrels and Guinness on tap and "uiske in the jar, boys."

This Festival of Fire celebrates all the Underworld Déithe and all the things and people we've loved and lost who are all living somewhere and in some way, and we dance with them between the worlds because it's easy at Samhain. This is the rite of the Bone Fires, when the bones of dead things would be burned to see the spirits of the living to the land of Tir na n'Ogh.

The Feast of Bride
(August 1; February 2 in the Northern Hemisphere.)

The Season of Winds and Ravens Talking Loudest.

This is surely the second battle of the seasons (the first being the Spring Equinox).

Mostly our winters are cold (although there's a young English "refugee" living in our garden in the old caravan who looks at us with dismay when we shiver).

Although in the middle of the day short sleeves can happen and clear blue skies are normal, everyone still complains and many people go to Bali. Then, just when everyone thinks we couldn't get any colder, the temperature soars and we can smell the scents of spring in the air and everyone heads to the water, strips, and gets a momentary tan. Two days of that and the thermometer will plummet. Every year it surprises us; every year we forget.

And then the winds begin and seed is spread—prelude to tomorrow's rampant growth. (I planted these five-inch high trees in my back garden on the Winter Solstice six years ago, and the highest is about forty feet high already, and the garden is now a rain forest!)

The ravens hold tribunals in the back lane beside the creek as they reassert their territorial boundaries with the new season's young. They know us in this house, following us all the way when we walk to town. Many of us bear the tattoo of the raven as our totem.

We celebrate the Feast of Bride with incredible abandon, because even though the jasmine is yet to bloom we know it's just about to happen, and the warm days change us all.

This festival celebrates fertility, virility, and vitality—Brighid and her beloveds, and Oengus Og (Lancelet), the Déithe of Love.

Beltane

(Around October 31; May 1 in the Northern Hemisphere.)

Season of the Orb-Spinner, the Cicada, Abundance, and Nudity.

And Beltane is just the beginning! All hail to the Déithe of the sun and the onset of warm days, the riches of in-season avocados, mangos, pawpaw, every living delicious food under the sun, when the jewfish are running and there's a barbecue out back with the music full-bore, and the beer and uiske beatha's flowing like gold under a warm evening sky.

The days of swimming are back, and the bodies are already brown all over; there are a trillion cicadas singing so loudly on some days that even when you yell at them to be quiet they don't hear you.

Visitors are told to beware walking in the garden after dark because the giant orb spiders are spinning their webs, and if you don't know where to walk (because the spiders certainly know where to spin their nets!) you'll find yourself screaming because you have no idea if it's on you or if you merely got "webbed."

And what began in abandon in September—tick season—is challenging everyone, as these tiny, venomous, blood-sucking uglies silently and easily dig into every tender, moist orifice; they drop on you from every tree and from every bush and from every blade of grass—from the almost microscopic grass tick to the cattle tick, the paralysis tick and the shellback tick.

This is the season when the people that the "civilized" call "Ferals" are up in the hills and deep in the forests engaged in Tick Wars, fighting each other over territories due to the large sums of money paid by serum laboratories for live ticks with their jaws intact (which can't happen once they've burrowed, as we have to break their jaws, without squeezing their poison sacks in the process, as we twist them counterclockwise to get them out of the terrible places that they enjoy so much).

This season celebrates the fair folk and all the High Kings and all the High Queens from the Dagda to Artu, from Mórrigan and Danu to the Ladies of the Lake.

The Other Celebrations

Winter: Our Winter Solstice marks the return of the ibis, and it's the time of quiet and working on the projects that we've left undone all through the warmer months.

Spring: September is the season when everything just grows rampant, and goannas and blue-tongues and frill-necked lizards, frogs, snakes, and creatures from the sublime to the insidious awaken and remind us we're no different from any other creature and less prolific, even, than many!

Summer: High Summer is blue-bottle season—the little ocean swimmer, so cute and seemingly innocuous floating like translucent blue sails on the incoming tide, with tentacles several feet long that wrap around your face and body and sting like nothing except the jumping jack (an ant that'll make the strongest among you turn to a quivering ball of mush). It is the return of the idiot season, when the tourists come from their chair-bound lives to dump their rubbish or break their bottles on the pavement because our town is supposed to be a cool place, and aren't you allowed to be an idiot in a cool place? But it's also the time when the birds call the dawn so vigorously that it's necessary to put a pillow over your head if you need to get a couple of extra hours of sleep.

Autumn: March is "wear-an-empty-ice-cream-container-on-your-head, or take-your-chances" season because the magpies bear their young and will attack anyone or anything within a hundred yard radius of their nests (and it's the other battle of the seasons, whereby a week of cold will challenge the soft, warm days for supremacy), and when the bats spend hours dancing and squawking on the tin roof over my bed, eating the guavas. Late sunset, into dusk, you'll see them in great flocks that fill the skies with the leathery rattle of their "wings," but in the mornings the wildlife rescue usually has their hands full saving them from barbed-wire fences—so much for sonar!

From Samhain to Samhain we celebrate the seasons of the earth! We share abundant feasts and copious quantities of glenfiddich or beer or mead or good red wine—the pleasure of each other's companionship, living and dead.

Wherever you are you need to be aware of the immensity of life and death and your connection to it all—not by way of book or authority, but because it's a part of you—and celebrate it, because that's what witches do.

Part 8

Attitude and Enchantment

16   No Light Without Darkness

Vulture, when you come for the white rat that the foxes left,
Take off the red helmet of your head, the black wings that have shadowed
me, and step to me as man: the wild brother at whose feet the white
wolves fawn, to whose hand of power the great lioness stalks, purring . . .
You know what I was, you see what I am: change me, change me!

—Randall Jarrell, "The Woman at the Washington Zoo"

Consider, for a moment, what life could be like both for you and for the earth if you could see and understand the patterns of change in their entirety, without getting caught up in concepts of time and personalization.

It is recommend that reflection on the "circular" rather than the "linear" will help you: all things within the known universe revolve around each other in ever-widening arcs, eternally and infinitely. Everything also emits in some energetic way or another. Circular concepts can be considered from the greatest in cycle (to the farthest reaches of unknown space) to the infinitely small.

Light and dark are to be considered in the same context.

Light is as infinite as darkness; they are relative; expansion can only be truly understood in its relationship to contraction. Certain schools of new-age thinking still attempt to disrupt the pattern of life by referring to the light like it was something pure and clean, and darkness as something inherently evil. I think it is important to question such terminology (including the construct regarding magic and witchcraft as either being white or black—these are decidedly biased and racist terms).

Nothing that you or I say or do, on our own, will change the destinies of those who seek to cause harm intentionally, despite personal or global consequences, but it is in this section that I wish to discuss the practical application of your Craft.

The Lost Years

The Forest Sauvage and the Search for the Grail

How hard has your life been before you embraced the way of the witch? Times of madness? Days, maybe years of lostness; not fitting in?

You're not alone. I don't know many witches who have not been to the place where the surface world did not bite the heart out of wonder, leaving the draíochta to wander in an alien landscape bereft of meaning. That's the secular world that is currently attempting to override, with its brutal reason and its demand for uniformity, the uniqueness of individuality and the ways of the sacred.

How many countries (other than Ireland) allow tax exemptions for the artist and still honor the poet as greater than the warrior?

That's what I call the Forest Sauvage—the savage forest.

And I'm not talking wildwoods and secret groves or wolves or bears or outlaws waiting to rob you of your purse, or your life, or . . . or am I?

The Forest Sauvage is your testing ground, wherever it is. You're trapped there, struggling to learn the rules of survival until you either give in, go mad, or get slipped the mirror that allows you to take the big risk. You can be there for years. Some never make it and succumb to a living death or a needle or a bottle. Some do all three and still escape—they get slipped the mirror.

The mirror could be another person who reminds you of your quest, or a book, or a film, even a certain kind of music—something that reminds you who you are and that there are others who think and feel as you do. The big risk is to make the break knowing you could fail. That's courage, and courage is only ever realized in the face of fear—of death, condemnation, loneliness.

The Forest Sauvage could be a vast city or a small country town or a religious family—poverty, uncertain peace, your sexuality, and peer pressure to conform.

You learn the arts of glamouring and of invisibility, forms of shapeshifting and certain tactics of battle. The Forest Sauvage will teach you that, and it *does* hurt you. Merlin went mad there, and so did Lancelet.

The infant Arthur is whisked away by Merlin, who takes him to live in a small kingdom in the Forest Sauvage:

> He is taught, by the Merlin, many things.
>
> He is taught to See, to Walk, to Listen, to Remember, to Learn for Himself. He is taught to Talk, to honour all things of the Sacred, to Defend Himself; He is taught the Power of Defending more than Himself. He is taught the Speech of Air, of Fire, of Water, of Earth, and he is taught to do with what He learns! He learns of the Sacred Places. He is given to understand the Instruments of Magic and how they are wielded. He learns about Beauty. He learns about Pain. He is taught Compassion and also Justice. He is taught to Question and to seek the Truth in all things.
>
> He is given the Power to keep open the Gates-Between-the-Worlds and to know which of Them is which!
>
> Not much more than a boy is He . . . but He is ready.
>
> —Ly de Angeles, from "The Pattern"

17   Scholar-Warrior

Demne twisted around and glared at the warrior.
"There is no room for honor in the heart that is filled with fear . . ."

—Diana L. Paxson and Adrienne Martine-Barnes,
Master of Earth and Water

The more you develop your connection with the world soul (Anima) and the draíocht associated with all that's here, the greater the impact of your actions and words on events both current and future.

There are far too many people sitting in armchairs reading about matters mystical and occult and extrapolating the information they have gathered for whatever reasons. There are many well-intentioned pagans, witches, and/or wiccans seeking both community and acceptance in the majority monotheistic cultures, and each person has his or her own work to do.

I am suggesting a very proactive approach to confronting discord, and I am suggesting that physical training and fitness be one of your disciplines.

I have been an initiated witch for over thirty years, and as an adjunct to a 100 percent involvement in the Craft, I now train *physically* as well as intellectually, psychically, and magically.

I had been rather sedentary during much of my adult life, focusing on the latter three disciplines and secretly knowing that the first was missing (I understand how easy it can be to let body-work slide when you have busy work schedules). Fourteen years ago I took up the martial arts again, along with other complementary training regimes, and as a result I experienced a sense of completion and readiness that I only thought I had. Truth is, I deceived myself.

When I studied the way of Tao and Shinto I spent a lot of time chuckling to myself, realizing that it's the sister to the magic of the "West."

It's all very well to work good practical magic, but I've come to realize that the terms "physical, mental, emotional, and spiritual" in relation to the disciplines of magic *do* involve more than herb lore. They mean "being able."

Most of my initiates, therefore, guided by my past inadequacies, work at a form of physical discipline—both the men and the women. I get called "Scáthach" by some of them, a title of which I am blatantly proud.

It may never be necessary, but history has a way of repeating itself, and I would ask you how you would defend your friends and family if your city or country were laid to siege? You could use the arts of invisibility and psychic protection to the best of your ability, and sure—that may be all you might end up requiring—but maybe not.

Earlier this year I was invited to attend a pagan summer gathering—one that has been operational for many years here in Australia. I've been so busy for such a long time that I had not attended a gathering outside my local area for almost twenty years.

When asked to attend I'd been asked what kind of workshop I'd like to present. Figuring that there were bound to be many pagans, witches, and wiccans who were already very certain in their crafts, I chose not to bore them with a workshop on any kind of magical theory or ritual but to teach the art of archery to those who wanted to learn. The administrators told me there was a huge interest, so I traveled to the gathering with two other initiates, both quite expert with the bow and both willing to bring their own bows to assist those wanting to learn (I'd also been put down to do a workshop on the martial arts stretch technique).

There were several hundred people there from all over the country, many walking around half-clad, as these gatherings are safe that way. But oh! Oh, my goodness!

The people who clustered around wanting to "have a go" at the shooting mostly could not pull the bowstrings due to lack of physical strength (please bear in mind that I weigh in at only 50 kg), and all but three (who have my deep respect) seemed to want to treat the instruments of our art like toys and found a great deal of difficulty in listening to what we were teaching, preferring to think of the instruments as light entertainment.

Many of the half-clad bodies reminded us of feta cheese, and I dared not do a class on the stretch technique for fear of the suffering I would cause.

We stayed long enough to have a very deep conversation with an Aboriginal Elder, who'd been invited to the gathering to teach about bush tucker and bush medicine, and who sat in the evening with just the three of us and quietly told us his horror story of being one of the "stolen generation." In case the reader is unaware of this several-generations-long event, it is a shameful legacy of an ignorant white bureaucracy that has yet to be righted by the governments and religious institutions of this land by the simple admission of its perpetration by the parties responsible.

After that we left the gathering (before the "Burn-the-Barbie" ritual that was to take place the following day to appease the obese in attendance— not that I have the slightest iota of respect for the Barbie doll or those who invented her and Ken!).

I have been in contact with very few witches who feel as my initiates and I do, and of those with whom I have spoken many have been verbally abused for their feelings on the subject, being told that paganism and witchcraft are peaceful religions and that there is no place for violence. To them I would say that the training as a warrior *is not violent*. It is an art of readiness; of preparedness of body, mind, reflex, and intuition; of strategy and the capacity to confront any circumstance.

The ability to be exceedingly calm and alert and very healthy are its gifts. Finding a good school with which to train, where honor is an essential aspect of the training, is recommended.

There is a group quite close to where I live whose members call themselves the Enemies of Rome. They excel at the techniques of Dark Age fighting, and include the arts of blacksmithing and resurrecting ancient traditional clothing, weaponry, techniques of working leather and dyes, and specialized equipment. The head of this troupe is also a Lao Di of Wu Chi Kung Fu.

A Word About Violence

The way of the warrior witch is not about violence, as I have just demonstrated. Violence is all about cowardice or thoughtlessness or sheer hooliganism; it's about the abuse of women and children, the bully who has something to prove because he's not good enough without the use of cruelty, the rape of resources, the industry that exploits its workers and dumps its toxins on land and in sea and into the atmosphere, the use of vivisection or the carelessness of humanity toward other species of life, the intolerance of the differences of others, the intentionally cruel word or condemnation based on uninformed opinion or elitism.

Violence is the violation of the right to live without fear, or the condoning of its actions through apathy, denial, or ignorance.

Ergo . . .

The way of the warrior witch is proactive, whether that be through peaceful protest or active participation in solutions to disharmony and, if it came down to it, the capacity to defend.

18   Shapeshifting

I am a wind across the sea
(I am) a flood across the plain
(I am) the roar of the tides
(I am) a stag of seven (pair) tines . . .

—Aisling, "Duan Amhairghine (Amergin's Challenge)"

Animal Totems, Linking Spirits, Therianthropy

There have been philosophic debates relative to what defines humanity (in difference to other life forms), and the main answers seem to be the continued assumption that our capacity to reason, express emotion, and, in some wacky references, our ability to conceive of "a higher power" duly marks us as being greater than the beasts (the "I think, therefore I am" notion was thrown out long ago).

The strongest argument seems to be humanity's ability to utilize innovative technology: the transformation of a thing, via a set or series of formula, ranging from the invention of clockwork to flight to laser technology, and the ability to comprehend and use symbolic complexities such as language, most particularly written and pictographic representation of symbol or meaning.

Why then is there so much suffering?

I think it's rather sad, really, that our supposed complexity has divested us of the ability to feed and clothe ourselves without several intermediaries between us and the product's origin. This could be considered as time and labor saving, but it certainly places us at a conceivable disadvantage should we ever find ourselves in a situation of necessary self-sustainability. I have often wondered at the ease of the bee or the elephant to feed itself and live its life with such seeming lack of debt or hustle or clock-watching.

Beastie!

The study of the behavior of animals other than us, and empathy and identification with them, is about reconnecting with the Source, and this has been a specialization of witches and shamans and sorcerers since time immemorial.

It seems that humanity is the only animal that kills for sport or entertainment, and that is due to the paradigm: "power over all the beasts of the field," and an elitist attitude that presumes that because we seem to do so many things differently, we are somehow better. As a consequence humanity is currently coming very close to "homo-norming" the earth. Homo-norming is allowing for only the foods we consume and that which feeds them to the exclusion or extinction of all else. *Uh, oh!*

The honor and emulation of other species is one of the hallmarks of draíocht. If we contemplate the concept that we may very well have been, at some stage of our evolution, in some great soup of one-celled life forms that diversified over a very long time for the sake of adaptation to changing environments and conditions, then it is also possible that at some level of the "evolutionary chain" we are related to every other life form (and variations of the theme) and that on a scale of one to ten we can envision wolf at ten and man at one, and a sliding scale of relationship between them. What, then, of the people who are at about six or seven on the scale? They have perhaps carried the memories of the diversification in their genome for billions of years, and their ability to relate to life, their instincts, and their capacity of response is determined by their ancient relationship.

We are as tribal a society as any other. Western culture is merely conditioned into believing that it is otherwise. We are mainly a social, communal animal, and always tend to form alliances with like-minded others, and when under duress or threat we revert to the "tribal-mind" very quickly (just consider the increase in street gangs). There are always the loners as well, and these people have links to certain other animals that more than likely exhibit similar qualities.

In cultures closer to the soul of earth, the recognition of the totemic animal, either individually or collectively, is a very sacred matter, and the idea of killing *any* animal for sport or entertainment is an impossible concept.

The idea of ingesting the attributes of the kill is also a time-honored one, and upholds the truism, "You are what you eat."

Being comfortable with who you are and knowing your own nature are at the core of the training of witchcraft. As such, you will, through observation and research, come to see yourself mirrored in at least one other creature, and through empathy, emulation, and Otherworld journeying you form deep alliances with the beast to which you are akin.

Sometimes it is easy to see the creature-ally on the faces or in the attitudes of others, but it is more difficult for us to see these things in ourselves, and it is a good idea to enjoy yourself through observation of the people around you.

Please remember to be wary of biases, because the pig and the boar and the rat are not to be denigrated, as I have heard some do. Just recently I was sitting around the lounge-room with the gang, and we were discussing each others' alter-animal attributes. One of the boys asked what I saw when I looked at him. Straight off, I said, "ferret." Initially he was put off by my comment, until he remembered being in a friend's house back in England; someone with a ferret had come to visit, and the ferret had fallen in love with him and had chosen to spend all its visiting time in his room. Hmm.

I'm going to list merely a few other creatures and their magical attributes. The exercise for you is to search out (not necessarily from this list) whichever creature is your own totem. Study its qualities and seek it out as an ally, for its wisdom and guidance, on your Otherworld journeys.

Invoking what each creature represents serves two purposes: it absorbs the attributes of your ally and enables you to take its shape, when necessary.

Your research and exploration are tantamount to your connectedness to a personal or "hearth" totem, and your ability to shapeshift.

Creature Totems

(Note: For a fully in-depth understanding of the nature of animal totems, please read *Animal Speak: The Spiritual & Magical Powers of Creatures Great & Small*, by Ted Andrews.)

Dragon

The dragon symbolizes the land itself, with all the hidden intricacies that are implied. Wherever the dragon is found in the Mythos of a people, it is considered both a creature of fertility and an unstoppable force. Dragons underground can represent deep disturbances; dragons in the air can represent weather patterns; dragons of the land represent the ley of the land and the trackways that are created as a response to the patterns of the creatures that walk them.

The dragon is a huge totem, and the person invoking its power should do so wisely. It is a formidable ally but a formidable enemy, and the people emulating its awesome power must be deeply calm in their own nature while realizing their capacity to respond to danger.

I mention it firstly to enable the practitioner to be both aware of its complexity as well as its strength, and to begin the list with the least approachable ally.

Just don't be glamoured by it if and when you discover it's your totem.

Salmon

The salmon teaches its ally how to get in touch with his or her ancestral knowledge and how to put it to practical use. It is an ally that symbolizes both knowledge and wisdom, and is said to be as old as time, and knows both past and future.

Any shapeshifter wanting to travel by water is likely to seek out the salmon.

Horse

The horse totem is many things: its qualities are majesty and justice, stamina, endurance, and faithfulness. Horses are sacred to many aspects of the Goddess, particularly Epona and Rhiannon, and they are linked to the moon, night, mystery, and draíocht. In all the legends there is no more potent companion, with the exception of the hound.

They are a loving and intelligent ally upon journeys into the Otherworld, and it is advisable to always heed the horse's warnings.

Hawk

As with other birds, the hawk is a messenger ally. It represents far memory and clear sight, and it will warn you of any upcoming situation that requires you to remain alert to possible danger.

Stag

The stag represents all that is regal. He is the symbol of personal striving and achievement, and the (natural) pride associated with how one conducts one's life. He is the definitive Otherworldly guide, particularly when seen as white, and can assist you to see the truth in all things. His appearance quite often precedes profound change.

Deer (and the White Doe)

The doe is a guardian of the forests of life (the day to day and the Otherworld) and is a messenger totem. She symbolizes all that is uncorrupted, and teaches you about sincerity and beauty. She can see right to the heart of any situation, and can soothe you when you are sad.

Bear

The bear is a great carer and a potent protector. It symbolizes the warrior spirit and will always herald an adventure. The bear represents longevity and is a teacher totem.

Owl

The owl is usually known as a messenger or representation of Cailleach, the wise woman, and is a very busy Otherworld guide. The owl is a night guardian and an aid during intense tribulation and times of loss or mourning. It is also said to represent the souls of the dead or to call a person who is due to die. The owl can aid you to unmask deception around you.

Raven

The raven is a bird of oracle and prediction. So often associated with the battlefield, ravens have received a grim reputation. The raven is one of my own totems, and I have found it to be the totem with the best sense of humor. The raven can find something positive in any situation. It is the great survivor, and its cunning is admirable! It can impart secrets and keep them. They are always Gatekeepers to the Otherworld, and are excellent and loyal in a fight.

Wolf

The wolf teaches its totem (you) how to pass by danger without being observed. It will teach you how to interpret the world of nature. It is an amazing teacher and will guard you from harm under any circumstances. The wolf is another of the most loyal of totems.

Fox

The fox is like the trickster and adapts easily to any situation. It is a totem of strategy, and will make certain that you are always fed. It is the master of observation, and can impart much value to the pupil who wishes to reverse trends of laziness.

Dog

The dog is the archetypal shapeshifter and has all the qualities of the wolf. Dogs are always companions in Otherworld journeys, and they can assist you to hunt out the guilty in a situation where you are uncertain of the facts. They can find lost things and people, both here and in the Otherworld.

Eagle

Known in Gaeilge as *Iolair,* the eagle is associated with leadership and integrity. As a totem it is associated with great vision and independence of action. The power of the eagle aids you in the guardianship of whatever you hold most sacred in the face of confrontation.

Wren

A very small bird totem, it is, however, held in high esteem. Its talent is outwitting even the most logical procrastination (even your own). It will guide you to recognize your own limitations and help you to overcome them in the simplest fashion. There is a legend about a competition between an eagle and a wren to see which could fly the highest. The eagle, at its greatest possible height, looked down through the air toward the land. Contentedly, it considered itself the victor, as the wren was nowhere in sight. The eagle felt a movement on its back and looked to see the wren nestled there quite comfortably.

Otter

The otter's curiosity reminds us that everything is interesting if looked at from more than one perspective. Otters know how to float on the currents of life, enjoying it. They remind you not to take things too seriously. They offer us the gift of laughter, trust, and playfulness. Otters glide through the emotional ups and downs of life with ease, and can teach you to do likewise.

Seal

They have the agility to move from anger to complete calm with ease.

Observation of this creature will teach you the same. It advises you to be mindful of your imagination and insights, and its gift is clairaudience and the capacity to heed your inner voice—it teaches you how to listen, and that sound is an inherent part of ones creative, imaginative powers.

Cat

Nine lives—the ability for quick recovery from distress or illness, and the ability to turn from being the victim in any situation to one of sleek realization.

The cat is a totem of a healthy curiosity, independence, cleverness, unpredictability, and healing. The actual kind of cat that becomes your ally (from tabby to tiger) is a variation of the same theme, and contemplation of how it appears to you leads to deeper understanding.

The cat is at home in the dark. It is a guiding ally in matters "supernatural," and can always sense nonhuman presences. Cats are fascinated by all things draíocht, hence their predominance as familiars. They sense "evil."

19   Keeping Records

I am forgotten until you remember me.
I am the living root; the forever tree—
I await beneath the senses for the soul who truly listens with an ear to
hear my mystery . . . and in the song of such a one I am remembered;
and remembering will set the sacred free . . .

—Ly de Angeles, "The Watcher"

The Book of Shadows

This is a handwritten book of preferred rituals.

You may take the rituals that others have worked on and perfected and use them for yourself, and may not ever seek to write your own. However, you must personalize them so that they really "fit" your true allegiances. Seek out the Esbats of the lunar cycles—the full moon, new moon, and dark moon—that honor the three faces of one aspect of the Goddess. There are the Fire Festivals of Samhain, the Feast of Bride, Beltane, and Llugnassad; and the solar rituals of solstice and equinox may need your personal touch. Record all other rites and invocations that are important to you, including banishings, fith-fathing, house/tuath-blessings, birth and death celebratory rituals, hexing rituals, and so on, in your Book of Shadows.

The Grimoir

This is your record of "what works." It is a recipe book of spells and lists and ingredients; your private book of specialization that may actually take years for you to fill. It may include herbals, candle magic, knot or cord magic, weather draíocht, what cycles of the month or year you have discovered to be most productive (even whether the times of the hours of the day or night make a difference), incense mixes for specific purposes, what oils or oil blends to use, why and when; all manner of successes. You can start out by including suggested recipes and spells that you might read about, but please be careful to check their validity.

A Diary

In your diary, record Otherworld journeys and their results, contacts or allies and the information they give you, pertinent dreams, explorations, and experiments.

A Library

Create a library of associated works, music, or artwork—things that inspire, are traditions of your own or another's, or simply that you feel are worth preserving and sharing. Other initiates, or your children or their children, could find this useful.

Part 7

The Law of Three

20 By Earth, by Sky, by Sea

Go n-éirí an bóthar leat
(May the road rise with you)
Go raibh an ghaoth go brách ag do chúl
(May the wind be always at your back)
Go lonraí an ghrian go te ar d'aghaidh
(May the sun shine warm upon your face)

—From an Irish blessing

The Healing Cycles

Even though it seems I have spent much time discussing the nature of "four," it is in accordance with certain patterns only. The nature of "three" is profound insofar as it represents the principles of life, generation, and regeneration in ceaseless revelation.

Ultimately, the principle is simple—so simple that some witches have said to me, "Surely it can"t be that easy." The thing about spellcasting is that what works does so *because* it is simple.

First, know that there is always before, during, and after, and that the pattern of working with threes also means that what you have wrought will take three days, three weeks, three months, or three years *if it is not instant*. The thing is that all successful spellcasting *is* instant, but may take an unfolding to become obvious.

A good example is the healing process: if a person gets hurt and the wound is not very serious, the process of healing begins instantly but will not be obvious for three days (as in the case of a cut or a bruise); with internal injuries or infections, the problem will normally clear in three weeks;

with broken bones—three months; with deep hurts, like mourning a loved one, the process can take up to three years before the hurting eases or stops.

There are three days to each lunar or solar festival—the day before, the day of, and the day after (just as there are three days to any major event). There is a three-day preparation period before an initiation (called the dead days).

Please remember this when casting spells—the outcome begins immediately, but you may not realize it as one of the cycles of three—I mention this because of what occurs, in many instances, after casting a spell. So often events seem to enter into a state of discord. This is *natural* and *necessary* because you are changing circumstances with your spell *that require circumstances to change* for the outcome to be attained (I realize this is "duh!" but you'd be amazed at the number of people who don't get it!), and therefore instilled patterns must be rearranged, often in quite a seemingly chaotic manner, before they can assume the altered pattern.

To Cast the Spell Thrice Times Three (Minimum)

Here's an example: the word "draíocht." Its very potency is in its simplicity, and the fact that I know (or *you* know, for your own purposes) what I am causing to happen as a result of the spell.

I begin by saying the one thing that will start the process:

> *See the door that hath no key*
> *Other than the way I go,*
> *Other than the name of me.*

And I'll repeat this three times. (The name, of course, is the draíocht name that you are known by only to your Déithe, other initiates, and yourself.)

Then I chant the enchantment:

> *The key to unlocking*
> *The door I want open*
> *Is hid in the depths of the mind.*
> *I can take it or leave it*

Or hum it or breathe it
The key to the door I shall find.
I have it before me
I'm holding the door-key
I turn it—this bond I unbind.

I'm going to repeat this charm at least three times, having learned it by rote beforehand. If I chant it more than three times I will speed up, ending with just shallow breathing until I become breathless. Then I will slow my breathing; relaxing and letting it go until I'm so relaxed I could easily fall asleep. Then it's done. To complete the spell I have my own personal verbal Triscele that seals what I have done. You must create your own— no one can do that for you.

The Purpose of the Plait

Sometimes I'll have a plait or two in my hair and someone who doesn't know me very well will comment. I recall when my friend Kate asked whether the plaits meant anything, and my daughter piped up with, "Oh, that's just Mum making plans!" (My offspring all grew up with the Craft all around them every day—very fey.)

There are many techniques for concentrating sufficient potency into whatever spell you are casting, but I have always found that the act of plaiting is the most proficient way of weaving something into actuality.

Magic, Myth, and Mystery (the Art of Magical Poetry)

(The Déithe teaching the student the art of poetry by way of the following axiom: "The key to the gateway is thrice times three, and thrice times three, and thrice times three, and thrice times three again. There is no gateway past ten . . . and thence on times seven.")

TEACHER: The Key to the Gateway is thrice times three?

STUDENT:

The hooded stranger:
His quest unspoken?
One white tree?

Some track untrod?

The name of a god?

The Piper's fee?

The five senses?

The wind at your back?

Earth, Sky, and Sea?

Is that it? And then what? No, wait, there's more! Another lock; another door . . .

TEACHER: And thrice times three . . .

STUDENT:

Fealty,

Bravery

Mystery,

Humor,

Honor,

Wonder,

Listening,

Questioning,

Challenging?

And then?

TEACHER: And thrice times three.

STUDENT: Okay, I've got it!

If ever there was a problem

That needed to be solved

Then looking within is where I first must go,

If ever there was something

That needed to be said

I better be sure I'm right in what I know,

If ever there is a journey
That calls for me to come
Then pack in case of unexpected snow!

TEACHER: And thrice times three again . . .

STUDENT: Um, can I use a conversation for an enchantment? (No answer from the teacher, so the student attempts it anyway.)

"I'm not finished!"
I say you are!
"Who are you to tell me!?"

Get out!
"Where can I go?"
I don't care and I don't know!

"Please?"
. . . this one time only!
"I'll begin again then . . ."

TEACHER: There is no gateway past ten, 'cause that'd be eleven . . . but then you've got the Gates that number seven!

STUDENT: Oh, come on! Well, alright . . .

Seven Gates go down, down;
They take your knowledge; they take your crown,
At each Gate challenged; they take your gown.
They take your name—take everything,
They take it all to save the King.
Meet the Mirror and mercy give,
They teach you, then, a way to live.

Is that it? Am I there yet? Will you *please* answer me!? (No answer.)

The Déithe chuckles, mumbling, "The Key to the Gateway is thrice times three: Time and Matter and Energy!"

Another hears him:

> "Shh!"
> "Oops!"
> "S'okay, I don't think she heard you."
> "Phew! Sorry!"
> "No need to be . . ."
> "'Cause there can't be more than just we three!"
> "Well, that's just how it's meant to be."
> "Where is our third god, anyway?"
> "Oh, she'll be back, you'll see!"

The above is a poetic play-around with some rather profound concepts that link the magical numbers into variations of expression: the four threes, incorporating both four (the need for strong foundations to any enchantment) and three (the principle of creativity); the sacredness of the number nine (as in the Witches' Ladder) in spellcasting—a number that represents the completion of anything and the inclusion of all preceding numbers from one; the number ten mentioned is the mystical understanding that ten is one in a transformed state (the zero now adding infinity to the numerical concept).

The number seven represents the astrological portals of experience (not including the Ambassadors of the Galaxy), as are represented in almost all descent myths.

Rhythm and rhyme are, together, a potent method of both remembering and projecting, as they tend to weave the spell into a tapestry in the Unseen-Real—rather than just wanting a thing to occur one creates the thing through the ancient poetica upon which verbal magic is founded.

The Little Triscele: A Blessing (Called: Thríbhís Beag)

At the conclusion of many invocations, at the close of letters to others of the Craft or affiliations such as druidry and wicca and paganism, I will often sign off with the Thríbhís Beag (little blessing):

By Earth, by Sky, by Sea . . .

You already have seen it at the conclusion of several rituals in this work. Other variations can be used when performing a house blessing, a healing, or at the completion of a benevolent spell:

> *By Earth, by Sky, by Sea*
> *Be ye blessed;*
> *blessed be!*

Again, a triple blessing, or:

> *I chant the spell to set it free,*
> *by the Earth, by Sky, by Sea,*
> *as I do will, so mote it be.*

All are variations of the same blessing.

The Great Triscele: The Bond (Called: Thríbhís Mór)

The Great Triscele (Earth, Sky, Sea) is an enchantment that is indivisible and is never broken down to three separate parts. It ensures your responsibility and vigilance. You are as responsible for casting this bond as the person so bound. While the enchantment itself is seen as a blessing and ensures well-being, it is invariably linked to one's geas. Breaking the geas, or denying it, is like breaking an oath with life itself.

An Thríbhís Mór is akin to a contract between oneself and another or oneself and one's Déithe, and backlash for the breaking of a geas acts as a whole (the sea rises to drown you, the earth opens to swallow you, the sky falls to crush you—or variations of *that* theme!).

When used as a conclusion to a hexing or binding or banishing, nothing seals it with such strength—be aware, however, of your responsibility when applying this. You really need to be very clear regarding your intention, and using an Thríbhís Mór for petty or personal reasons is bound to produce a backlash. Someone would have had to get away with cold-blooded murder (or similar), because invoking an Thríbhís Mór is like summoning the Wild Hunt.

21   Three Years and Three Days

She sail'd it round, and sail'd it round,
And loud, loud cried she—
"Now break, now break, ye fairy charms,
And set my true love free!"

—Sir Walter Scott, "The Lass of Lochroyan"

The Three Main Functions

The three lines of training are similar to the concept of first, second, and third rite, but these functions are not representative of ascending grade, as is usual in traditional wiccan or magical groups; they are "Deepenings," and your alliance will eventually be with one or more of the three.

We find that the whole hierarchical thing becomes very much a bain insofar as, like it or not, when a hierarchical training regime is the acceptable practice (as in any other hierarchically-based cabal or organization), ambition or position can override the quality of the group's potency. An adept coven is like a circus troupe—everyone is individual, working together like something well-oiled. The seeming head (high priesthood) is responsible to the others within the group, due to years of involvement and expertise, to ensure that the individual members are given quality training, and that all relevant material is available to the initiate for his or her development. The witches that work with me are always on alert for any inadequacy or hypocrisy, in either each other or myself, because complete trust is required between us so that no draíocht is adulterated by either ineptitude or egocentricity.

Many of the initiates that I have trained over the years choose not to take the position of high priesthood, preferring, instead, to remain affiliated with our coven in the role of elders, because in our branch of the Craft high priesthood is recognized as a major responsibility, and we only take it on when we are prepared to hive off to form our own coven and accept—and teach for a minimum of three years—new initiates, being aware of the following: that in truth, the training and learning of an initiate never stops.

I fully maintain that it takes a good ten to twenty years before the "Deepenings" have hit bedrock.

The Green Line (First Year—First "Degree of Application")

The training and growth achieved here reflect your awareness of the earth as supreme provider. The Green Line ascertains that you're "in touch" with the anima.

Other than the personal interaction that you will undertake with the elements and their guardians, with the rituals and invocations of each of the Déithe, you'll also make or procure each of the ritual tools, and come to understand the many processes necessary for their consecration and use.

The other undertakings of the Green Line are all associated with the earth and the physical/magical arts of the Craft, such as the work of a healer, herbalist, husbandman, ecologist, and environmentalist—any and all skills (other than your job if you've got one) associated with craft and land and animal. Include within this year the pattern of learning about, and eating, healthy food, and acquiring a physical discipline if you've not already done so.

Listen to the weather; become aware of the subtle changes that mark the seasonal progressions, and get to notice things like when the Huntsman (that's a spider) comes into the house, knowing that she'll do so when rain is coming. Come to know the most auspicious times for planting and reaping your own foods by the cycles of the moon. And study both your own and other species for similarities.

Do your Otherworld journeys and establish good connections with your totem(s) and familiars.

Work your rituals to sun and moon and element and season to "deepen" your core pattern as a working witch, and begin your study of myth and legend and comparative spiritualities.

The symbol of the Green Line is the pentacle.

The Red Line (Second Year—Second "Degree of Application")

Becoming fey with the Dragon and the draíocht of earth is the first step; at the same time I am really aware that witches are usually of an artistic temperament—it kinda comes with the territory, so to speak.

The Red Line are those initiates who are involved with the arts in whatever fashion, but this degree of application includes a sound knowledge and understanding of the mysteries of draíocht gained through study of the legends and mythologies associated with your priesthood.

You may choose to look at the psychological implications of archetypal analogy—the effects of magic on consciousness, and so on.

Red Line witches are upholders of the lore of what's sacred. They work the rites to the earth, moon, sun, and star, and apply their training through the lineage of the Merlin (or Morgan le Fey); they are the musicians, the poets, the talkers and storytellers, the writers and the artists who express to others by way of both art and science, and so they keep magic alive.

Due to necessity they often remain in standard occupations or lifestyles (with a tendency to attempt to find a way out), while still working their Craft.

Their symbol is the staff.

The Black Line (Third Year: Third "Degree of Application")

The witches who have come to learn of the great earth as provider and who have found their specialized talents in this field—those who have learned of the rites and rituals of their Craft, the myths and mysteries of the ways of the sacred, and the arts most natural to them, will eventually come to dwell at the thresholds that link the world of the day to day with all others. They are most comfortable being between-the-worlds.

They can't be other than "different" and will not be found in mainstream lifestyles. They seek to live well, however they can—sometimes with great difficulty—in an often-hostile world, until such time as their talents support them. They are often involved in oracle and prophecy, and will have trained sufficiently to enable them to fulfill their geas with the Déithe through either example, teaching, or both.

These initiates will have established themselves within Imramma by way of constant journeying between the worlds, and they work hand in glove with the Déithe in the unfolding of the patterns of forever. They are either high priesthood or elders, and should be sufficiently wise in the ways of draíocht as to be in the position to pass information to students to enable them to also re-establish links with the ancient future/past.

Their symbol is the sword.

Epilogue

He lies upon his bed with his arm flung over his eyes, thinking deeply about the feeling—no, the certainty—that he really had no choice; that taking upon himself the mantle of witch was more a calling. He is so "connected" to these so-called "old gods."

He lies wondering about who he is and just where this *really* began.

He breathes deeply and rhythmically, attuning his racing mind to the music of his own body, as he attempts to silence unnecessary thoughts that interfere with his quest.

He seems to sleep . . . not many would know that he does not.

He is listening for me . . .

The Watcher

I am long forgotten. How is it you have heard?
Do I still sing upon the wind of Now? Is that it?
Who listens? Who listens still? The hand that holds me on a cold
and frozen heart? The voice that keens lament for the lost?
The forgotten also?
The apple that was not plucked

and therefore fell to seed against the need?
A pattern in the clouds?
The meaning of the raven
when he seems to speak of matters so important?

I watch them come—the wanting ones—the song within them
deep and calling something . . .
I watch them go—empty—because they
thought I was their own
voice—but I wasn't!

Oh, keep me warm . . .
the bells within the mist; the flowers on the shrine;
the moon within the darkness of a disillusioned mind;
the ruby in the wine;
the legends lost to time . . .
the ancient song.

I am long forgotten but you hear me.
Do not despair for you are not just you, but "we."
Let them go. Hold not to hope of others being "kind."
But let yourself remember . . .
the ash beside the brook, the sacred in a look,
the empty pages of a book.

Who knows why you perceive me in your sorrow—
for who am I that in that place I dwell?
Well . . .
It is in the Way of the forgotten that in
the silence of your sadness
strange faces rise to haunt you to remind you
that you're listening for the host and for the piper
and for the harpist of a dream. Catch my song?
Within the whisper of the wind within the trees
upon the lost forgotten shore?
Everything is still here.

I am forgotten until you remember me.
I am the living root; the forever Tree—
I await beneath the senses for the soul who truly listens
with an ear to hear my mystery . . .
and in the song of such a one I am remembered;

and remembering will set the sacred free
to walk through dreams that can rebuild the ancient trackways,

to awaken memories of fires on the hills,
to call the faidh and the ceoltóiri to attend me
As I plant the living legends in the places of the deep,
(where the forgotten ones still sleep)
of the forest of profusion of the ever-living Tree.

I am the Watcher of the Gate—I am not found
in any book already written, already printed, already bound
but in the spaces yet to be heard;
in the mystery of the yet-to-be-written word.
Ancient Now. Alive divine.
Prepare a place for me; a face for me.
Deny me not; I am the legend of the Vine
And I am yours, beloved—you who hear me
And in an act that holds to nothing, we entwine.

—Ly de Angeles, "The Watcher"

Daily Rites

The Witch's Day Begins at Sunset

It's advisable to set up, at sunset, by lighting a simple stick of incense and a candle, getting focused, and acknowledging that all that has occurred before this day is *gone!* That with the coming of the night a whole new series of experiences is possible. It's important not to become complacent with your life—to view it through continually "innocent" eyes.

The most auspicious times of the solar day to work are at sunrise, mid-day, sunset (particularly sunset). These are times of transition (similar to the triple cycle of the moon). They are not necessarily times of ritual, more of opening up your awareness to the forces of the waxing and waning of the day.

The process of awareness is such that you will be breaking down the usual time barriers of a common daily routine.

At any one of the times mentioned, a simple invocation will suffice, mainly as acknowledgment of the Déithe with which you resonate.

When you work this rite at dawn—and if your day allows—it's always good to go back to sleep, even for just an hour. The dreams that come to you after an intentioned waking can be significant. Write them down; they can be among the most intense that you will experience.

I acknowledge the Light to the World! Blessed N . . . be with me!

(N . . . indicates the name of the persona of Déithe that you've invoked.)

Linking with the tide of the solar day is an acknowledgment of the Déithe of life and the cycles of life (sunrise: birth; midday: the prime of life; sunset: the wisdom of life's experience; midnight: death and transformation).

Set aside five minutes around noon, and either meditate silently or walk in whatever natural setting you can find.

A simple invocation would be:

I invoke the Déithe ar draíocht! N . . . be with me!

The third aspect of the solar day, sunset, is to be treated as your descent into the Underworld prior to a new day (the womb of the night produces the new day). It is the secret tide, the time to switch off from all problems, to reassess what has occurred for you during the past solar day.

Again, keep the invocation at sunset relatively simple:

N . . . I invoke the fiàin draíocht (wild magic),
and the art of Silence!

B As the Cup is to Woman . . . ?

(This article is dedicated to the memory of Marion Bradley,
who died September 25, 1999.)

All witches, within ritual, place the blade of their athame into a chalice of wine in a known act of consecration.

This consecration is understood to be a symbolic sexual act that acknowledges the communion of our Goddess with her Consort, both of whom are represented by those participating in the ritual.

Yes and no.

There is much more to it—much more—and a deeper understanding will assist those among you who have experienced the knot in the belly; the small (or not so small) warning bell of apprehension that may or may not be consciously acknowledged.

Over the years, witches that I have worked with have pointed out a variety of dilemmas of conscience concerning the consecration of the wine. Some have felt that the very concept is a brutal and violent symbolism—some have refused to practice this tradition, preferring to use the wand—until the deeper significance of the ritual was told to them; some have found the symbolism decidedly sexist.

With a more profound understanding of the symbolism involved in the consecration of the wine you need never consider the process *during* ritual, as the deeper understanding is transferred into the consecration itself. A powerful event is realized: communion with life itself!

And, being thus, the words of consecration become superfluous.

There are four things to consider: the chalice, the athame, the wine, and you. I will cover the actual and symbolic significance of each (where applicable).

You

First thing to realize is *that* you are. And not only *are* you, you are *also* an outcome.

Within every cell of your material body there exists the patterns of for-ever—your mother and father, their mothers and fathers, what they may have been *other* than men and women in the far and ancient "past," what they may have been *before* they were *other,* going back to, one could sur-mise, the "Big Bang" (if one thinks in a linear fashion, and allowing the possibility for such a theory while, of course, allowing that things could be very different when considering any conceptual "beginning," and also allowing that beginnings don't really happen—things simply change from one thing to something else). Within every drop of hemoglobin dwells the iron (the *same* and *continuous* iron) that would have always been—suns and stars and space beyond. Therefore, you are the *Imramma* (soul-jour-ney) of your ancestors, and they are whatever it took to create the pattern of your physical form in the now.

You are the outcome of a deep and ancient forever.

Your understanding of this is paramount; your knowledge of who you are is merely the tip of the whole truth. You actually dwell in the lifescape of forever, which can be accessed through the vision of the imagination (a potent place). This is the "Unseen-Real."*

We are, however, *other* than simply a material presence, and we can create other than biological children, as have our ancestors, as *all* acts of creativity are acts of creation—are children after another fashion—and all inventions and realizations are also children, after another fashion.

Goddess and God (that which we consider as Déithe) know us and are known *by* us in the lifescape of the Unseen-Real (like the pattern within the seed).

The Wine

This is the Legend of the Vine, the Tree of Life, in the Seen-Real. The wine is from outside ourselves (is that truly so?), and it *is* the blood of the fruit of forever. When we *do* drink of it we drink deeply of the blood of the fruit of forever. It is the communion of the Unseen-Real with the Seen-Real, and as such it is like sex with one's beloved.

The wine, also, is a forever thing and has its own Imramma that disappears into the deep and ancient "past." (Please note that I place "past" in emphasis to leave open the question of its viability as an "anything-at-all" if all things that have ever been are inherent in the "now").

The Chalice

The Chalice represents the vessel in which life is held (as also is the individual holding it). Symbolically it resonates with cauldrons, wells, sacred pools, lakes, wombs, the matrix of anything; life itself that holds all life within itself—a very sacred thing, you would agree.

---

* This could also be considered "the Mythago," "Annun," "that-which-is-beyond-the-Veil," and "the Archetypal Realm."

The Athame

The Athame is known to be an extension of the initiate's will. The athame is traditionally made of metal *because of the alchemy involved in the process of its creation.*

The witch dedicates his or her life to the way of magic—the way of the sacred—and to live life to the fullest. A witch's work is to live consciously.

To live consciously we are aware of our actions, of the ramifications of those actions, and of the patterns that individuality perpetuates within the lifescape that we call Creation Continuous. Much (of mind, body, imagination, response) takes place. This training takes place both within the sacredness of a coven, grove, or temple, *and* within the lifescape of the day to day. Both are of equal importance.

To train ourselves away from the conditioned responses of a concrete and secular culture can be very difficult, and can mean much misunderstanding and, at times, devastating loss.

This is the meaning of the alchemy of the creation of the athame: from the ore to the crucible, from the crucible to the forge, from the forge to the anvil where hammer blow by hammer blow the dagger becomes.

By fire and water and air is the material reality changed and shaped—transformed—into something utterly unrecognizable to what it once was. But, oh, there is so much more to it . . .

- The *blade* of your athame is double-edged and tapers to a finely-honed point.

- The *hilt* is considered as separate, but connected, to the blade.

- The *whole must be balanced* to the hand.

One edge of the blade represents *compassion,* and the other, *severity.* This is the clear ability to distinguish *yes* from *no.*

The hilt represents our intent and is, therefore, representative of us in the Unseen-Real and *who* we are through all the worlds.

The *balance* is what is most important to us—the balance of realization; of living; of how we think; how we respond; the "rightness" (or otherwise) of any act of ritual or spellcrafting; the balance of our intent . . .

. . . and the *point* is the union of the Unseen-Real with the Seen-Real.

Realize that the athame represents *you* in the Seen-Real so that when you consecrate the wine within your chalice the union of the *four* parts forms a whole. What is the whole? The consecration itself!

When you drink of the wine you enter into a sacred union with life itself, both in honor of the ancestors (and the gods) of the Unseen-Real, and in honor of the ancestors (and the gods) of the Seen-Real.

This is the meaning of communion.

This is why the consecration of the wine is the most sacred of sacred acts.

To *consciously* partake of the forever Tree of Life leaves us with no doubt of the continuum of all things, that there is no such thing as "death," and, having drunk the wine, that the Seen-Real and the Unseen-Real meet, in the body and blood of the Initiate.

So . . . during ritual, when consecrating the wine, words become superfluous when the knowledge of the act, combined with the act itself, produce such an awesome understanding.

Between the Seen-Real and the Unseen-Real exists the Veil; the Mist; the Threshold; the Gate-Between-the-Worlds—the "place" where magic happens. It is only known by knowing it.

To Ride the Tiger

A couple of years ago I gave a group of students an assignment for the week. They were to search very deeply and come up with their own unique opinions about what love is.

On the following Saturday each read aloud what they had written, being very careful to give lots of esoteric, deep, and mystical descriptions.

I said, in my Sagittarianly tactless way, that they'd all cheated. I promised them that I'd come back the following lesson with one of my own descriptions.

To Ride the Tiger (*On Love and the Wild God*)

If I talk to you about love, then what?
Shall I be truthful sometimes—most of the time—
and lie to you about this?
I could, but I won't. Just this one time I will tell you.
To know love is to know fear.
My capacity to be rational, to be objective, to be detached,

to be alone—all gone.
I am mad. I am destructive. I am consigned to
some kind of all-consuming chaos.

It's the Wild God.
From the depths of "somewhere" he soars into the
world of the Seen-Real.
And who knows where he wanders; who else sees him also?
But when he looks out at me through this man's eyes and I see him?
And when I am invited to the Dance?
Well . . .
And all through it I know the man I love is mortal—is just a man—
though never just like any other man, for I see the Wild God in his eyes.

So I ride the tiger—and that's a wanton, awe-inspiring ride!
And all the while that I ride it's like some ancient primal dance
to the burning, savage, erotic tune that the Wild God plays,
And my instinct says to fear.
Truth be told, I live and dance with the Wild God in the Unseen-Real
all the time—for when does one not think of love?
And sometimes I think that all my years of magical training and
discipline have been about being able to Dance with him as an
equal, not simply as a mortal.

And still this can cause me to fear because I wonder, now,
if I can love a mortal man.
I certainly can't do it the way I hear of other women doing it—
I'm too proud.
I'm not able to be "nice"; I'm not able to pretend
to be other than what I am.
So mostly I'm very guarded.

I am most guarded when I see the Wild God in your eyes,
because I know the Dance in the mortal realm

. . . and when it takes place here it also crashes through all the worlds
and drops down and down into the Underworld—the savage forest
within the depths of the Dreamtime of magic, its Source, its Mythago
Wood—breaking all the nets of delusion in the fall.

Sometimes I dare.
I stand at the Wild Wood Gate, in my little cottage garden, and I dare
him to come through the Mist and into the open, because I know what
he yearns for also—
And perhaps with training, through honesty of body, soul, and spirit—
perhaps, once upon a time, I can meet
him without anyone getting burned.

You knew it, didn't you, when I asked you the question, "What is the
essence of love?"
You knew I was talking about this—this rapture, this thing to be
feared—and not trees and children and friends and books and ideals and
music and food?
Yes, we all know that we can love this way.
We all know how passionate and safe and tragic and joyful and distant
from the Core are these loves.
We know we can remain ourselves—remember our mortal identities—
with these loves. We may even choose to die for the right to freedom, to
defend our children, to preserve a way of life—
. . . but with all these faces of love we have a choice.

The other kind of love?
The depths of the rapture of the wild embrace with
something that's Divine?
No choice when we let it in.
No choice but to ride the tiger.

And some people have told me that I'm a cold bitch,
that I'm the Ice Queen.
They don't realize how contained my own wildness is.

And that the wildness is all about love—to enable me to be at one with

the tiger when I ride; to not have to think about it;

to realize that the tiger is not my enemy.

To finally, ultimately, naturally,

Enjoy the ride.

D The Matter of Deity

Dear Ly,

I wanted to ask you a quick question though (as always).

I read something recently that was attacking the idea that the gods are internal to each individual, and that they were most definitely external, real, individuals (in the individual sense). I have tended to view this whole "situation" by thinking on two different levels. I accept the separateness of gods from one another (and me), on the same level that I accept that you and I are different people. Obviously this is an important perspective, as it is the way that we naturally live and view the world, and also allows us to commune with gods on another level as friend, lover, parent, and even child (etc).

Having said this, however, I accept that fundamentally all of the distinctions that I draw are arbitrary, and everything (including gods) is part of one big "mess," which I now call life (a product of our discussions).

Is this the way in which you understand life and the gods? I think about it and I wonder to what extent this second method of viewing the world (as one big thing) is relevant. I can't actually look at the world this way; it's just not how it appears to me. But I cannot get rid of this idea (and consequently don't want to). It sings to me so deeply. It makes all of the rest make sense. I am also reminded of the conversation we had where you told me about a conversation where you told someone talking to you that they where looking at god, and that this idea was not egocentric but humbling.

I also remember that I couldn't sleep that night, having lost my protective blanket, and fears racing through my mind.

When dawn came though, and each day after that, I realized that you where right, and that everything was still the same, only my understanding had changed.

This is a side issue, but the experience of trying to process all this stuff has left me with a firm understanding of the way in which each of us is everything, and thus completely responsible for ourselves and the world that we live in.

I guess my point is that at this stage I don't and can't understand the gods as something radically separate from myself. I cannot do away with my second level of understanding. I guess I'm just after your impression of what I have said.

Sorry to lump such a huge email on you, but I enjoy constructive (or destructive, which is usually only constructive in a different way) dialogue.

Much Love & Blessings,

Tom

The Reply

Bright blessings Tom,

I've sat on your last letter for a while.

It's really hard to answer this one! It's just that I don't know, really, how to explain anymore. I once could.

A long time ago I would have said, "No, the gods are definitely outside of me; independent of me despite the fact that I am of them," but then there was once upon a time when I could also consider them as archetypes—real and yet symbolic of something inexplicable.

And yet; and yet . . .

Now, when I seek to explain, I think that *any* personification is limited by the limitation of human awareness. I especially consider that personification of the "divine" is the grossest of aberrations, as the group entity that is humanity is flawed (not intrinsically, and certainly not naturally), and therefore to consider the gods in humanity's image, either from a considered "ancient past" or as an ideal (relative to humanity), is to render the gods in an obscene garment.

If I consider individuality (in contradiction to the group entity), then, yes, I can see, sometimes, something sacred shining "from within" them.

But if the gods are an inner thing and that inner thing is taken as a generic, then they're fucked, because (as a generalization) humanity's fucked.

When I read and contemplate the way of empathy of many tribal cultures, I feel a sense of mirroring that the millennia of monotheism could never mirror. I sense those millennia of monotheism almost like the viral invasion of a living organism (humanity) with itself (and its dogma), as though the thoughtforms have become an entity that is eating our world through its host (humanity).

So I don't go there. I give it no energy—nothing of myself.

Mostly I have spent my life fighting this entity whenever I encounter it (as the agent of other gods), and it has the heads of gorgons and it shows itself with the face of many doctrines and each one is capable of feeding this entity, that people call god, by blackmailing people with promises.

There's a war between gods. I really know that to be so. The gods of the living earth and the entity (perhaps plural) that that virus has created through the enforced indoctrination ("By way of a hostile sword"—Bede) and over a thousand years of persecution and brain-washing.

I'm on a bit of a study quest to find the source—so far it seems to stem from Persia, but something (someThing) must have whispered it into being and then perhaps was not been able to control it (fucking Magi and their demonic evocations!), because ever since Zoroastrianism introduced the concept of "light" (sorry, "LIGHT") and "dark" (sorry, "DARK") as distinct from each other, introducing dualism into consciousness, we've been TOLD how to worship, and hence have lost "grace."

And so life suffers.

How does one close Pandora's box?

Ah. But . . .

I hear the song of a different divine. Always have. I don't have to name them because they haven't got names—names are for anchoring; for ease. The fight for life seems to require that they remain as anonymous as possible, known to those who feel them and who are content to represent them in the form of whatever bodies—two legs or four, winged, finned, none at all, engrassed, entreed, enstoned, enrivered—whether soil or sand, wind or lightning . . . truth be told I sense with every pore that nothing lacks awareness and that all things are of the gods (our gods), but . . . that these gods are not of all people, as they probably had to let go of the one's too far gone with the virus—they've joined the entity, and, therefore, the entity is legion.

What bothers me the most is that the entity is like the cane-toad.

Anyway, Brother Tom, I'm mailing you a book. It's called *The Wood Wife,* and I consider it *profound.* Make note of what Tomas says about what we are discussing here.

I know you know.

All my love,
By Earth, by Sky, by Sea,
Ly

Glossary of Unusual Terms

Amhairghin

("Amergin," as usually spelled in English). He was one of the leaders of the "Men of Míl," who battled the Tuatha dé Danann for possession of the island. He was renown as a sorcerer and a bard.

Bodhrán [bowran]

Traditional Irish drum.

Brighid [brih-ed]

One of the greatest of the goddesses of the Tuatha dé Danann. Poetry, healing, and smithcrafting are under her auspice. It has also been suggested that Brigantia, the goddess worshiped by the Brigantes tribe of Northern England, is analogous with Brighid. Some derivations of her name are Bride and Brigid, and her sacred day, also known as Imbolc, is called the Feast of Bride.

Breo-saighit

The Tuatha dé Danann name for Brigid, meaning "fiery arrow."

Connaught
The west of Ireland.

Déithe [day-ha]
Gods (plural/multiple).

Deosil
Sunwise.

Draíocht [dree-uckht]
Magic. (Draíochta: magical.)

Dram
A drink, usually pertaining to uiske beatha (whisky).

Fáilte [falcha]
Welcome, happiness.

Fiàin draíocht [feeya dree-uckht]
Wild magic.

Fíanna [feena]
A wandering band of warriors.

Filì
A poet.

Filíocht [filyucht]
A variation of *filì*. Poetry; verbal magic ("word draíocht" is verbal magic).

Fionn Mac Cumhaill (Finn MacCool)
Legendary Irish warrior possessed of every skill.

Gaeilge (Gaelic)
The language of the Gaeillge people. "Gaeillge" refers to the Gaelic people.

Geas [gaysh]

The law of the geas is similar to a spell that is either placed on an individual by self, others, or the Déithe. We are not necessarily born with one or more of these spells, but can accrue them throughout our lives. Once recognized, they are best heeded, because to break a geas is to bring misfortune to self or other. They are not considered as curses or taboos, but rather as draíochta obligations.

It can be such that it is a bond between self and the Déithe or self and one's oaths and they can seem quite weird: if one eats a certain food, it will break the geas; if one says a certain word or phrase, it will break the geas. They are not always apparent, but you will discover it sooner or later because when you repeat certain things and the effect is blatantly awful; you soon recognizes it for what it is. It is akin to the understanding of "karma." It is also known to be spelled "geis."

Imramma

(Also called Imram.) "Wonder-voyage"; a way of describing forever and our connection to it; voyages to Otherworlds. The Imramma is based upon a certain fundamental understanding: the voyage represents the passage into the Otherworld, the testing of the soul, the journey into and beyond death, and the empowerment of the spiritual quest.

Meán Earraigh [myawn ah-ri]

Spring Equinox.

Meán Fómhair [myawn fohw-er]

Autumn Equinox.

Meán Geimhridh [myawn gev-ri]

Winter Solstice.

Meán Samhraidh [myawn sow-ri]

Summer Solstice.

Mórrigan, Macha, and Badb [More-rigahn, Makka, Beeve]

Traditional triad of the Crow or Raven Goddess.

Ogham [ohk-am]

A form of writing used by the Druids; an oracle. Named for Ogmios, patron Déithe of eloquence, communication, poetry, learning, and scholarship.

Palingenesis

The continuous unfolding of one's life by way of the inhabitation of many bodies; one's genetic blueprint; the pattern of the tree within the seed.

Quicken Brew

A brew made from the berries of the Quicken Tree (said to impart immortality), and planted nowadays only in remote and secret places. A draíochta rowan tree.

Red Branch

The Red Branch was a band of warriors in ancient Ulster led by the famous Cú Chulainn, considered by some a myth, by some a god. His name meant "Hound of Chulainn," and he is a stunning example of courage, honor, and loyalty.

Reiving

An archaic term that I was told of when I was young—it indicates a form of banishing of unwanted energies by way of intentional cleaning. Got it from my grandmother, who, in context, used to always say, "There's nothing as clean as a witch's kitchen!" and, "Leave no corner dark."

Scáthach [skaw-hakh]

Her name means "The Shadowy One." She lived on the Isle of Skye, where she had a school to which the greatest of Ireland's warriors came to be trained. Cú Chulainn was one of her students, as were many other Red Branch warriors. Scáthach did not train women because of a Celtic belief that maintained that only women could teach men effective battle skills, and only men could teach them to women.

Scéalta [skaelta]
Stories.

Seanachaì [shan-ukh-ee]
Storytellers.

Sídhe [she]
Also known as faerie and the fair folk (as in bàn-sídhe, Pict-sídhe).

Slànte! [slahn-sha]
"Cheers" (also "goodbye"). *Slàinte go mhile fàilte* [slansha go mila falsha] ("good health and a thousand welcomes") is a major greeting and welcome.

Teamhair [Tara]
"Place of kings." The most important socio-political sacred site of pre-Christian Ireland to both mortals and the Tuatha dé Danann.

The Folk
The descendants of the Tuatha dé Danann.

The Lost
Humans who are naturally draíochta.

Thomas the Rymer
Thomas the Rymer was a famous fourteenth-century Scottish prophet. It is said that he gained his powers of prophecy from a meeting with the Queen of the Underworld. He traveled with her for forty days and forty nights into the Underworld, and served her for seven years. He then returned to the Upperworld endowed with the gift of a tongue that cannot lie. He is thought to have returned to the fair realm. He is said to be a mediator between this world and the Otherworld. This is a role he serves with other figures, such as Merlin.

Thríbhís Beag [treevis byog]

A three-fold blessing (also a sacred island off the coast of Ireland—one of three).

Thríbhís Mór [treevis moor]

The great Triscele of earth, sky, and sea (also a sacred island of the coast of Ireland—one of three).

Tuath [too-ah]

Means both tribe/people of the territory and the territory/countryside in which they dwell.

Tuatha dé Danann [tooah day danahn]

The people/land (sometimes called "the children") of Danu/Dana/Anu.

Uilleann pipes[illen pipes]

Three hundred years ago the uilleann pipes were played in both Ireland and England, but are nowadays exclusively Irish. They differ from the bagpipes insofar as they are made of leather and have dry reed rather than wet. They are played in a sitting position. An extremely specialized instrument.

Uiske beatha [ishka baha] (Fire-Water)

Whisky.

Widdershins

Against the direction of the sun.

Recommended Reading

Alexander, L. *The High King Holt.* New York: Rinehart and Winston, 1968.

Anderson, F. *The Ancient Secret.* Orpington, Great Britain: Aquarian Press, 1987.

Anderson, W. *Green Man.* London: Harper Collins, 1990.

Andrews, T. *Animal Speak: The Spiritual & Magical Powers of Creatures Great & Small.* St. Paul: Llewellyn Publications, 1993.

Ashcroft-Nowicki, D. *The New Book of The Dead.* London: Aquarian Press, 1992.

Ashe, G. *Kings And Queens of Early Britain.* London: Methuen, 1982.

Bancroft, A. *Origins of the Sacred.* London: Arkana, 1987.

Barker, D. *Symbols of Sovereignty.* Newton Abbot: Westbridge Books, 1979.

Bellingham, D. *Celtic Mythology.* London: Apple Press, 1990.

Best, R. I., and O' Bergin, eds. *Lebor Na Huidre: Book of the Dun Cow.* Dublin: Royal Irish Academy, 1929.

Blamires, S. *The Irish Celtic Magical Tradition.* London: Aquarian Press, 1992.

Bond, F. B. *The Gate of Remembrance.* Wellingborough: Thorsons, 1978.

Bradley, M. *Mists of Avalon.* London: Sphere Books, 1984.

Bryant, P. *Awakening Arthur: His Return In Our Time.* London: Aquarian/Thorson, 1991.

Bulfinch, T. *Bulfinch's Mythology*. 3 vols. New York: Modern Library, 1991.

Caldecott, M. *The Green Lady and the King of Shadows*. Glastonbury: Gothic Image, 1989.

———. *Women In Celtic Myth*. Rochester, Vermont: Destiny Books, 1992.

Campbell, J. *Masks of God: Occidental Mythology*. New York: Penguin Books, 1988.

———. *Masks of God: Primitive Mythology*. New York: Penguin Books, 1987.

———. *The Hero with a Thousand Faces*. 2nd ed. Princeton, NJ: Princeton University Press, 1968.

———. *The Way of the Animal Powers*. London: Times Books, 1984.

Coghlan, R. *Pocket Dictionary of Irish Myth and Legend*. Belfast: Appletree Press, 1985.

Conway, D. J. *Celtic Magic*. St. Paul: Llewellyn Publications, 1990.

Cooper, J. C. *An Illustrated Encyclopedia of Traditional Symbols*. London: Thames & Hudson, 1979.

———. *Symbolic & Mythological Animals*. London: Aquarian/Thorsons, 1992.

Cross, T. P., and C. H. Slover. *Ancient Irish Tales*. New Jersey: Barnes & Noble Books, 1988.

Cunningham, S. *Cunningham's Encyclopedia of Magical Herbs*. St. Paul: Llewellyn Publications, 1985.

Darrah, J. *The Real Camelot*. London: Thames & Hudson, 1981.

de Angeles, L. *Genesis: A Legend of Future Past*. Byron Bay, Australia: Wild-Wood Gate, 2002.

———. *The Feast of Flesh and Spirit*. Byron Bay, Australia: WildWood Gate, 2002.

de Chardin, T. *The Future of Man*. New York: Harper & Row, 1969.

de Lint, C. *Forests of the Heart*. New York: Tor Books, 2000.

———. *Someplace to be Flying*. New York: Tor Books, 1999.

Dillon, M., trans. *Cycles of the Kings*. London: Oxford University Press, 1946.

Duncan, A. *Celtic Christianity*. Dorset, Great Britain: Element Books, 1992.

Eisler, R. *The Chalice and the Blade*. London: Unwin, 1990.

Estes, C. P. *Women Who Run with Wolves*. London: Rider, 1992.

Farrar, S., and J. Farrar. *Eight Sabbats for Witches*. London: Robert Hale, 1981.

Flint, K. *Challenge of the Clans*. London: Bantam Press, 1987.

———. *Champion of the Sidhe*. London: Bantam Press, 1986.

———. *Riders of the Sidhe*. London: Bantam Press, 1987.

Ford, A. *Isis: Afrikan Queen*. Somerset, Great Britain: Capall Bann, 2000.

Gimbutas, M. *The Gods and Goddesses of Old Europe*. London: Thames and Hudson, 1974.

Gleick, J. *Chaos: Making a New Science*. London: Heinemann, 1988.

Graves, R. *The White Goddess*. New York: Farrar, Strauss & Giroux, 1966.

Hawking, S. *A Brief History of Time*. New York: Bantam Books, 1988.

Hooke, S. H., ed. *Myth, Ritual and Kingship*. London: Oxford University Press, 1958.

Jung, C. G. *The Archetypes and the Collective Unconscious*. Princeton: Princeton University Press, 1981.

———. *Man and His Symbols*. New York: Doubleday, 1964.

Kharitidi, O. *Entering the Circle: the Secrets of Ancient Siberian Wisdom Discovered by a Russian Psychiatrist*. San Francisco: HarperCollins, 1996.

Llywelyn, M. *1916: A Novel of the Irish Rebellion*. New York: Tor Books, 1998.

Matthews, J., and C. Matthews. *Mabon*. London: Arcana, 1990.

———. *The Western Way*. Vols. 1 and 2. London: Arcana, 1986.

Mór, C. *The Moon on the Lake*. Sydney, Australia: Random House, 1997.

———. *Scratches in the Margins*. Sydney, Australia: Random House, 1996.

Murray, M. *The God of the Witches*. New York: Oxford University Press, 1973.

Paxon, D. L. *The White Raven*. New York: Avon Books, 1989.

Quinn, D. *Beyond Civilization*. New York: Three Rivers Press, 2000.

———. *Ishmael*. New York: Bantam Books, 1995.

———. *My Ishmael*. New York: Bantam Books, 1998.

Reanney, D. *The Death of Forever*. Melbourne, Australia: Longman Cheshire, 1991.

———. *The Music of the Mind*. Melbourne, Australia: Hill of Content, 1994.

Redgrove, P. *The Black Goddess and the Unseen Real*. New York: Grove Press, 1988.

Restall-Orr, E. *Druid Priestess*. Wellingborough, Great Britain: Thorsons, 2001.

Richardson, A., and G. Hughes. *Ancient Magicks for a New Age*. St. Paul: Llewellyn Publications, 1989.

Scott, M. *Irish Folk & Fairy Tales.* Omnibus ed. London: TimeWarner Books, 1992.

———. *Irish Myths & Legends.* London: TimeWarner Books, 1992.

Spence, L. *The Magic Arts in Celtic Britain.* London: Ryder & Co., 1915.

Squire, C. *Celtic Myth and Legend.* London: Gresham Publishers, 1905.

Starbird, M. *The Woman with the Alabaster Jar.* Santa Fe, NM: Bear & Co., 1993.

Starhawk. *The Spiral Dance.* San Francisco: Harper & Row, 1989.

Stewart, R. J. *Earthlight.* Dorset, Great Britain: Element Books, 2001.

———. *Power Within the Land.* Dorset, Great Britain: Element Books, 1992.

Sun Tzu. *The Art of War.* London: Shambhala, 1988.

Tepper, S. *Beauty.* New York: Doubleday, 1991.

———. *Family Tree.* New York: HarperCollins, 1998.

———. *Gibbons Decline and Fall.* New York: Bantam Books, 1997.

Torjenson, K. *When Women Were Priests.* New York: HarperCollins, 1995.

Walker, B. G. *Woman's Encyclopaedia of Myths and Secrets.* San Francisco: HarperCollins, 1983.

Watson, S. *The Kadaicha Sung.* Ringwood, Australia: Penguin Books, 1990.

Windling, T. *The Wood Wife.* New York: Tor Books, 1997.

Recommended Web Links

Timeless Myths

http://www.timelessmyths.com/celtic/index.html

This site is extensive and well worth several days of your time. It is devoted to Celtic myths and is divided into three sections:

- The Otherworld contains references of the Celtic deities, from Irish and Welsh literatures, as well as deities from ancient Gaul and Britain.

- The Warrior Society contains information on Celtic characters, particularly on heroes and heroines, rulers and other minor characters that appeared in Celtic myths.

- Celtic Cycles are filled with stories of adventures and tragedy.

Bernard Casimir

http://celtic-casimir.aunz.com

This site is well worth quite a lengthy study. The artworks are, unbelievably, all done by hand. Bernard Casimir is an artist, astrologer, poet, philosopher, and wizard of the first order (and he lives at WildWood Gate with the rest of us!).

Following is a quote from his writings on the Four Elements:

> The traditional four Elements are no longer treated seriously by the contemporary, discursive intellect which is uninterested in the world of symbolism. Well that's just too bad, 'cause symbolism is the focus here. Four (Elements) is what you get when you raise duality to the power of itself, what I like to call "four Cornerstones laid by Fate and Chance." Fate and Chance, destiny and free-will . . . Either-Or? Neither-Nor?
>
> But first, what is duality? Well I can tell you that it is not dualism . . .

Witchcraft Spells and Magick (at Branwen's Cauldron of Light)

http://www.branwenscauldron.com/witch_wicca.html

A quote from this site:

> How many times have you seen a sentence start with "Witchcraft, or Wicca, is . . ." leaving the reader with the impression that these are one and the same thing. Such generalizations are unfair to the practitioners of both, and more than a little confusing to those who wish to learn some form of the Craft.

Ly de Angeles

http://www.lydeangeles.com

Labyrinth: the author's website.

The Witches Way

http://www.witchesway.net

This site is directed to both the seeker and the initiated witch. Starrfire provides a broad spectrum of relevant information, contact, education, and commentary. She is both the creator of this beautiful site and a dedicated priestess of the Craft.

Witchcraft, Wicca, and Magick

http://www.lavenderwater.tripod.com

Witchcraft and other occult traditions.

LadyHawke

http://www.janih.com/lady

Another down-under witch, LadyHawk has heaps of attitude.

The Witches Voice

http://www.witchvox.net

Witches Voice links and networks witches, pagans, and magical traditions worldwide. Be sure to look up "Pagan Traditions . . . An Overview of Belief Systems."

Welcome to the Crossroads

http://www.summerlands.com/cgi-bin/index.cgi

A quote from this site:

> In the past, The People would meet at a crossroads for hospitality, ritual, or a gathering. In keeping with the traditions and ways of our ancestors, we offer you the hospitality of The Summerlands here at this Crossroads.

Mezzofanti: On Ireland and the Irish

http://www.mezzofanti.org/irish.html

A quote from this site:

> However, the natural isolation of Ireland and the tactical advantage of the Scottish highlander Celts made these groups virtually immune to enemy penetration—giving the Gaels in Ireland a unique chance to continue to develop their culture nearly undisturbed.

The Henge of Keltria

http://www.keltria.org

A quote from this site:

> We are a positive path Celtic Neopagan tradition dedicated to protecting and preserving our Mother Earth, honoring our Ancestors, revering the Spirits of Nature, and worshipping the Gods and Goddesses of our Gaelic heritage. Our focus is on personal growth

through the development of mind, body, and spirit. We place special emphasis on spiritual development fostered through study and practice of the Druidic Arts, or "Draíocht."

Imbas

http://www.imbas.org/

A quote from this site:

> Three things from which never to be moved: one's Oaths, one's Gods, and the Truth. The three highest causes of the true human are: Truth, Honor, and Duty. Three candles that illuminate every darkness: Truth, Nature, and Knowledge—Traditional Celtic Triads.

Nemeton

http://www.homepages.nildram.co.uk/~fealcen/nemeton.htm

A quote from this site:

> You have entered the cybergrove of Falconstowe: a site of personal Celtic pagan writings (or indigenous insular—i.e. British and Irish—pagan writings), with especial emphasis on Gaelic paganism.

House Shadow Drake

http://www.shadowdrake.com

A quote from this site:

> This website includes many resources which may be of interest to the general Heathen community. This includes information about traditional Witchcraft, Celtic folklore, herbalism, arts and crafts, history, and of course a wide variety of household sponsored resources for networking with the wider Heathen community.

The Meadows of Elfhame

http://www.angelfire.com/wy/elfhame/meadows.html

A quote from this site:

> This page is a virtual journey into the weald of Traditional Witchcraft. Herein, you will have the opportunity to learn authentic Traditional Craft beliefs and practices and to hear Inner Teachings of the Old Persuasion.